Time Management: Discover The Secrets to Beat The Clock

Learn How to Be in Control of Your Time, Maximize Your Day, Boost Productivity and Still Have Time to Enjoy Your Friends & Family

Table of Contents

Introduction 5
Chapter 1 – Stop Wasting Time 9
    The Importance of Time Management 9
    Signs You're Failing at Managing Your Time 11
    The Reasons Why You're Failing 17
    7 Big Myths About Time Management 19
Chapter 2 - Getting Things Done 101 21
    Essential Tips for Getting Things Done 21
    Essential Rules for Successful Time Management 23
    5 Lesser-Known Productivity Hacks You Need to Know 29
Chapter 3 - A Guide to Goal-Setting 37
    All About the Goal-Setting Theory of Motivation 37
    Goal-Setting Principles 38
    15 of the Best Tips for Effective Goal-Setting 45
    8 Common Reasons Why To-Do Lists Fail 48
Chapter 4 - The Secrets of Productivity 52
    How to Prioritize When Everything Is Important 52
    The Chunking Technique for Making Your Goals Achievable .. 60
    5 of the Biggest Productivity Killers and How to Overcome Them 65
Chapter 5 - Dealing with Distractions 68
    The Difference Between Internal and External Distractions ... 68
    Types of Internal Distractions 70

13 Ways to Silence Internal Distractions 74

6 Reliable Ways to Defeat External Distractions 80

Chapter 6 - Emulating Success 83

Goal Setting Examples from The Business Masters 83

13 Time Management Hacks of Successful People 86

10 Morning Routines of Groundbreaking Entrepreneurs 90

Chapter 7 - Regaining Control of The Future 94

15 Effective Time Management Habits 94

Defeating Perfectionism Once and for All 99

Tools and Techniques to Take Back Time for Good 104

Conclusion 110

Introduction

The only resource you can't barter, buy or borrow is time. It doesn't even follow one of the fundamental laws of supply and demand: high demand causes supply to increase and meet the demand. While we all have access to the same amount of time each day —1,440 minutes — we use our time differently.

Your success or failure in life depends mainly on your time management capabilities. To be successful, you need to invest significant amounts of time to achieve your goal or improve your weaknesses. At certain seasons, I spent more time than my competitors so that I can have the edge over them in the marketplace. I didn't assume that I was mentally superior to my competitors; I only spent time more effectively to balance the playing field.

You need to spend balance the time you spend at home and the time you spend at work. If not, you will be successful in one and be a failure in the other. Fear not; this book will show you how to balance your work and home effectively. I congratulate you on investing in your life and success by reading this book.

If you are reading this, it's probably because:

- You want to be confident that you can take proper care of yourself and your family
- You desire long-lasting success in your career and personal life
- You want your friends and families to be proud of you and your accomplishments

Here's what you're probably doing right in your life:

Since you are serious about improving your life experience, you are possibly implementing these basic career success strategies:

- You ensure that your performance at work exceeds the expectations of your bosses
- You arrive early and when needed, work overtime
- You are continually improving yourself to improve your work performance
- You seek mentors and network with your peers

The truth is, none of these actions will lift you to the personal or professional lifestyle you desire and deserve. Why? Let me explain:

For all things to function correctly, there has to be a balance. Let's use the washing machine's spin cycle as an illustration. When there are too many towels on one side of the tub, it slams, bangs and vibrates. If you don't fix it in time, the bearings will break, and the repairs can be expensive.

Your life can be likened to the washing machine. If you only focus and implement the necessary success steps of most people, you will achieve the same level of success as them. Thus, you may never accomplish everything you want or need in life. Your life will be completely imbalanced.

Over time, you will start getting drained spiritually, physically and emotionally. Consequently, you may begin to experience social problems, relationship problems, and health problems such as depression, diabetes, heart diseases, and high blood pressure. When you continuously live a life out of balance, you may never achieve your set goals or ambitions.

For centuries, the Chinese have known and have been implementing the yin and yang principle. The principle states that "two halves that complement each other produces wholeness." The keyword here is "wholeness." The two halves are your mind and your body; they work together to make your life whole.

If your life is not whole, you are not different from the wet towels swinging around the washing machine.

Let me tell you a secret: every successful person you have met and will ever meet are masters of productivity. If an expert should hand you the complete guide to success through proper time management, would you implement the steps in the guide?

- Will you use the secrets to increase your productivity and raise your success level?
- If you discover the productivity secrets of the most successful people, will you implement these secrets?
- I am willing to show you exactly what I do daily to consistently achieve my career and personal goals to live the kind of lifestyle you seek. Are you willing to follow these steps faithfully?

If your answer is yes to these three questions, then, you are ready to reach a new level of success with *Time Management: Proven Steps and Strategies for Managing Your Time Efficiently and Effectively.* This book

- Isn't just some rah-rah cheerleader guide that excites you with biographies and quotes of successful people. You won't find the typical "secrets to time management" that are copied and pasted articles from the internet and thrown together like some cheap pulp fiction novel.

- Details my exact daily actions and by all means, I am a successful and fulfilled person
- Shows you how to prioritize when everything is important
- Delves into the techniques for making your goals achievable
- Takes you deep into the biggest productivity killers and how to overcome them
- Helps you with ways to silence internal distractions
- Tells you reliable ways to defeat external distractions
- Contains goal-setting examples from the business masters
- Discusses time management hacks of successful people
- Takes you deep into the morning routines of groundbreaking entrepreneurs

I won't call this book a life-changing book. I will instead call it a life-enhancing book. With it, you start with the life you've built and elevated it to the levels you desire by implementing the exact steps of truly successful people.

In this book, you will find the precise information you need. You can start from the first page or read on topics that cause you the most challenge. I can assure you that this book will help you to maximize the scant 24 hours we all have per day.

For instance, you can check out chapter one for signs that suggest your time management sucks! Also, in chapter three, you will discover common reasons why you can't do anything with your to-do lists.

The point is, regardless of the chapter you choose to start reading, you will discover lots of valuable steps you can implement. Thus, you can increase your performance without increasing your work hours.

Chapter 1 – Stop Wasting Time

The Importance of Time Management

By definition, time management is a process of organizing and planning your time between specific activities to achieve efficiency.

Time is valuable to us whether or not we assign a dollar value to it. Think about the number of times you complained about having insufficient time to reach a goal or complete a task during this past week. If you don't fully understand why it's crucial for you to manage your time better, then, taking measures such as downloading time management apps, creating lists or adjusting your sleep time won't help you to solve your problems. First, take a look at the big picture to understand what you will gain from managing your time effectively. Here are eight critical reasons why you need to manage your time effectively:

1. Prevent procrastination

You leave no room for procrastination when you practice proper time management. You will become more self-disciplined as you become better at managing your time. Thus, you can become self-disciplined in other areas of your life where you lack discipline.

2. Find the time to relax

Due to family responsibilities, errands and jobs, the majority of us don't get sufficient time to relax and unwind. We struggle to find just 10 minutes to sit down and do nothing. With proper time management practices, you will get more done during the day and create the time to relax, unwind and prepare for a good night's sleep later in the day.

3. Avoid stress

It's easy to feel rushed and overwhelmed when you are not in control of your time. Thus, you will start struggling to complete your tasks. Imagine you were making frantic efforts to finish a project to avoid missing a close deadline. Then, your boss drops a new job on your desk and asks you how soon you can complete the new task. What will be your response?

However, when you can manage your time, you will complete most projects before their deadlines. You can adequately estimate the period you will use to complete a task and be confident in meeting deadlines.

4. Take advantage of learning opportunities

You become more valuable to your employer as you improve your repertoire. But if you don't have the time to enhance your knowledge, how can you become more relevant to your employer? Once you practice excellent time management skills, you can take advantage of great learning opportunities around you.

It doesn't mean going back to obtain additional certificates. Learning can be as simple as volunteering to host your company's open house. It can also be having lunch with colleagues in other departments to gain further insights into what they do. When you have adequate knowledge about your company and your industry, you have a higher chance of moving up the corporate ladder quickly.

5. Be in control of your life

Rather than following others blindly, time management allows you to control your life the way you want it. Thus, you make more sound decisions and accomplish more every day. Hence, the leaders in your industry will start seeking your help to get things done. With this increased exposure, you become perfectly placed for advanced opportunities.

6. Improve your decision-making

Regardless of the time management techniques you adopt, one significant side benefit of good time management practice is that you start making better decisions. When you don't have the time to consider your options before making a decision, you jump into conclusions and make poor decisions. Through effective time management, you feel more in control and can thoroughly examine your options before making a decision.

7. Improve your focus

When you are in control of your time, your concentration improves, and your efficiency is enhanced. Thus, you can complete your daily tasks quickly and effectively.

Do you want to consistently complete more tasks than anybody else? Do you seek promotion or awards? Then, you need to find the means to manage your time.

Signs You're Failing at Managing Your Time

Do you:

- Constantly have more to do than the time to them?
- Not rest from the time you wake up to the time you sleep in the night?
- Always feel tired after each day's work?

One vital attribute of a skilled manager is effectiveness. If you intend to accomplish a goal and you are not completing the right tasks to accomplish that goal, you won't accomplish it.

Here are some of the most common signs that you're failing at managing your time:

1. No task delegation

You need to identify tasks that you can delegate, automate or outsource and remove them from your workload. Here are examples of tasks that you can delegate:

- Your most time-consuming tasks. These tasks could be customer research, developing a marketing strategy, collation and presentation of data, traffic generation and improvement of click-through rate.
- Tasks others might enjoy. You may have become bored with a task after completing it repeatedly. Hence, if you think some of your colleagues could enjoy it, delegate such task to them. Also, if a colleague should volunteer for a task, allow him to perform it.
- Tasks in which teammates have better skills. Devote your time to other things and allow teammates with better skills to handle tasks that suit their skills and abilities. Avoid being the competition for your teammates. If they are better at a task than you, let them have it.
- Fun tasks. Your teammates are likely to take offense when you perform all the enjoyable tasks and ask them to deal with the tedious tasks. Why keep the fun to yourself? Let them share in the fun.
- Regular tasks. These are recurring tasks (weekly or monthly) and things that must be done after completing a project.

2. Agreeing to everyone

If you continuously agree to do things for everyone, excluding your loved ones, you won't have the time to improve your life or have the time for your loved ones. If you're always helping others without working on the important tasks assigned to you, you will constantly have an excessive workload. Being assertive and learning to say "no" is one of the best ways to improve your time management.

While it is great to help your teammates at work, it should only be an occasional occurrence. If it becomes a regular occurrence, you're doing their job for them and no longer helping them. They need to figure out how to work without continually requesting for your help. Otherwise, they also have time management problems, and they need to deal with it fast.

3. Indecision

Have you experienced spending lots of time to consider various options but still can't make a decision? It is a sign that you have poor time management. This sign is related to having ill-defined goals. When your goals are clearly defined, you have a basis for choosing your next most important task at any given time. The next task is often chosen based on the ROI. For example, assuming you are to choose between two 1-hour tasks. Task A will give you an ROI of $100, while task B will provide you with an ROI of $150. If your goal is to make more money, your obvious choice is task B.

Tasks vary in time of execution and costs. Also, you may have restrictions on the next task to be performed due to resources available, energy levels and other factors. After a clearly-defined goal, here's one question you can ask to make an easy decision on the next task to perform. "Using the time and resources currently available to me, what's the most important task I can complete?"

4. Perfectionism

When tasks take too long to achieve or even fail because you wanted to ensure that everything is perfect, you are a poor time manager. When you are overwhelmed by the need for perfection, you fail to realize that very few tasks are performed flawlessly in reality. By making unrealistic demands from your teammates, your desire for perfection can destroy your relationships with them. If you berate your colleagues when they fail to reach your perfect standards, you will struggle to find colleagues willing to work with you.

Since you can't maintain cordial working relationships with your colleagues, you will always have time management problems. You can't do everything by yourself. You should realize that perfection is impossible and, most times, unnecessary. Only demand the best from your colleagues for each task. Then, using the feedback from completed tasks, you can make the necessary improvements.

Bear in mind that a perfect job that never gets completed is useless compared to an average job that meets the deadline.

5. Productivity decline

When you manage your time poorly, you miss deadlines; you have an increase in backlog and your productivity declines. Time management and energy management are equally important. If you can't do anything with your energy levels, merely organizing your time is a waste of effort. Once you have reduced energy levels, you start having poor time management. Hence, you are under intense pressure to complete tasks without missing the required deadline. This even sucks up more of your energy levels.

Track your energy levels when you struggle to find the cause of your poor time management. Seek ways to improve your energy management.

6. Ill-defined goals

You can only prioritize when you have clearly defined goals. Consequently, you can complete your tasks on time. Each goal should have a clearly defined outline - what to achieve, when to achieve it and the order of importance. You need to set clearly-defined goals around your schedule of activities. Thus, you gain clarity on what needs to be done and when you need to do it.

According to the 80/20 principle, not all tasks carry equal importance. On average, 20% of your efforts will be responsible for 80% of your results. The smallest percentage of the tasks you perform will be responsible for the most significant percentage of the results you will achieve. You can only identify the 80/20 tasks when you have clearly-defined goals. A side benefit is that you will eliminate time-consuming tasks.

7. Finding excuses

The pressure of failing to meet a deadline makes you impatient. Hence, you start finding reasons for failing to complete your deadlines. Most people attribute their poor time management to people, technology or both. But the truth is, if you have failed to manage your time correctly, people and technology cannot help you. Ensure that you are only working on essential tasks that you can complete using the time and resources available to you.

You will ruin your ability to focus on the crucial task by adding an unneeded deadline. Assuming there is a task that needs to be completed by the close of business tomorrow, but you decided to shift the deadline to close of business today without being pressured to do so. You would only be putting yourself under unnecessary pressure and rushing to complete the task. While on the contrary, it would have been best for you to spread the task's process between today and tomorrow.

8. Hastiness

When you rush tasks, it is a sign that you don't have enough time for these tasks or meet the expectations of these tasks. While some tasks require some rush, you shouldn't be rushing to complete all your assigned tasks. You should have ample time between tasks to deal with unanticipated circumstances.

For example, a previous meeting exceeded its allotted time. If you leave every task to the last minute, you will continuously be in a rush. What you fail to realize is that if meeting A runs late, meeting B will start late, and you have to spend your rest period to complete your assigned task for the day.

9. Tardiness

When you can't allot sufficient time to appointments or tasks, you are unable to complete these tasks or fail to meet appointments. Your peers assume you are irresponsible. In some cases, your tardiness may be a motivation problem. You can't motivate yourself to get out of bed and do what you're supposed to do. One primary reason for your motivation problem may be a misalignment between your goals and your time management objectives.

Your best option is to prioritize your goals and manage your time to achieve these goals. When you schedule a goal that isn't your priority, you lose the motivation to be punctual since you fail to realize the importance of the task. Hence, you come up short at tasks without feeling any remorse, and you're known for your frequent poor time management practice.

The truth is, when you are punctual, it shows you respect your colleagues. The reverse is also true: when you are late, it is a sign that you disrespect your colleagues. Rather than being late for tasks that seem unimportant to you, you can decline to undertake the task.

The Reasons Why You're Failing

There are times we struggle to control our daily affairs despite our best efforts to efficiently organize our time, stay ahead of schedule or complete tasks successfully. Rather than creating additional to-do lists, you must identify the source of time management issues. Where is your time slipping away, and what are you doing wrong?

Let's take a look at eight reasons why you're failing at time management:

1. No plan at all

You need a proper method to change something already in motion in your life. Don't expect everything to fix itself. Create a timetable that makes you accountable for every hour of your day. Don't deviate from your daily plan, refer to it and review it. Thus, you can start developing and incorporating new habits into your day.

2. Procrastination

Start implementing your scheme immediately. Don't wait for the new month, Sunday or the next milestone in your life before making a change. The main idea is for you to act on the plan.

3. No grace

Since you're not perfect, there are times you will mess up. However, it doesn't mean you're a failure, or your hard work isn't paying off. So, give yourself the grace to get up the next day and be better.

4. Lack of accountability

Ask a trusted colleague to make you accountable for your daily actions. If you are late, mention it to the trusted colleague. Then, make a plan for what happens when you fail to meet your set expectations.

5. No motivation

The comments from your coworkers shouldn't motivate you. Decide on your motivation and ensure it's the right kind of motivation. Examples of strong motivators are personal development, excellence and well-being. Changes you make for your well-being will become a lifestyle change, but changes made for someone else won't last.

6. Making unnecessary changes

Concentrate on one specific goal at a time. If your objective is to get to work on time, identify the cause of your lateness to work. Then, eliminate it. Make it a priority to determine the necessary changes you need to make. Making unnecessary changes won't lead to new habits. For instance, spending two hours on Facebook early in the morning can cause you to be late for work. You can switch that up and spend two hours on Facebook the previous night. If the changes are necessary, make them a priority.

7. Unrealistic expectations

Don't over-expect. If you usually wake up at 7:45 am and get to work by 8.15 instead of 8 am, then, you can't suddenly start waking up at 5 am. It won't work that way. Your best option is to start learning how to wake up at 7 am. Then, slowly work your way up till you start waking up at 5:30 am.

8. Implementing a lot at once

One big mistake when addressing an issue in your life is to make a long list of things to change. Then, trying to take action on all these things at once on the next day. That's an entirely wrong approach. Your first step is to learn how to get out of bed on time. Then, seek to achieve the next goal. Over time, you would have developed new habits.

7 Big Myths About Time Management

In today's always-on business world, time management is crucial than ever. Though most professionals offer various tips to prioritize and balance work tasks and the home front, most of these tips are myths and poor advice that could have a negative impact than a positive one.

Here are the top seven myths you shouldn't buy about time management:

1. "Budget your time."

Don't be surprised when your budget gets shot 15 minutes into the day. Instead, create regular chunks of time in which you will make sufficient progress before moving to the next goal. During these chunks of periods, don't take calls, answer emails or check your social media page. Doing this helps you to avoid random interruptions rather than 'got a minute' meetings.

2. "Plan your day."

This was the mantra of time management. However, you may never get close to your long-term goals by using daily plans. Why? You finish each day with additional to-dos which you add to the next day's list until you give up on your long-term goals. A simple and effective solution is to include your long-term goals into your weekly plans.

3. "A detailed task list is essential to manage your time."

It is more important to structure your tasks in line with your strategic objectives rather than just listing them. You can become a master of time management by using 15 minutes before your bedtime the previous day to plan your next day to meet a defined expectation. You increase your decision-making and productivity by limiting your planning time.

4. "A structured day means a well-managed time."

For optimum results, time management, efficiency, effectiveness and productivity depend on each individual. There is no one-size-fits-all proposition. You need to find out what works for you.

5. "There's always time for your priorities."

You can still feel stressed despite knowing your priorities and aligning your activities with them. Bear in mind that you can only change how you feel about the time you have, but you can't change the time. It will always feel stressful to think you have insufficient time. Instead, tell yourself, "I have all the time I need to accomplish my desires." by doing this, you are more present and open to new, different solutions, you become more present and feel calmer. Thus, you can get more done.

6. "Schedule your hardest tasks first."

A recipe for procrastination is to attempt a tough task when you are rock bottom energy levels. If your energy is typically high at midnight, focus on the most challenging projects during this time. If you're usually flat on Thursday afternoon, schedule less important meetings for that day.

7. "Better time management is a result of better task management."

Though I am a fan of time blocking for managing priorities, I still believe that we need to make intentional choices on where to focus our energy before we can have proper time management. Since our choices define our priorities, we need to make better choices to have better time management.

Chapter 2 - Getting Things Done 101

Essential Tips for Getting Things Done

Getting things done, or GTD, is a reasonably simple method contrary to what you may think. It involves using simple rules to manage a few lists. Anyone, regardless of their background, can understand and apply these rules.

However, you need to develop at least one of the three habits for getting things done. Hence, the complicated part of GTD is in practice and not getting things done. Here those three habits:

1. Keep your head empty

"An empty mind is open to everything and ready for anything." - Shunryu Suzuki

David Allen is the author of *Getting Things Done - The Art of Stress-Free Productivity.* He recommends that you need to capture the essential elements necessary for you to get things done. Then, keep it out of your head in a reliable system where you can review it at any time.

Everything here includes what you have to do soon or someday (the big things and the small things). Some may be part of your work, while others may be part of your personal life. However, they should be the ones you regard as the most important and the ones you consider as less important.

Here are six reasons why you need to include everything:

- All things require your steady and conscious attention.
- You waste time and incur stress when you think of the same things repeatedly. Once you put them into a trusted system and out of your mind, you do them effortlessly.

- You have clarity on the number of things you need to do
- Since you are not distracted by indefinite stuff in your mind, your concentration increases.
- You can reject the things you shouldn't, and don't want to do since you have a clear idea of your commitments.
- You can start using your mind for creative activities rather than trying to remember things.

2. Be decisive

"When there is no next action; there is an infinite gap between current reality and what has to be done." - David Allen

Change is inevitable whether we like it or not. Hence, you need the discipline to decide the next best course of action. You must have a clear idea about your commitment to each activity. Then, make a decision about such a thing.

For your organization to work smoothly, you must empty your inbox regularly. Define and clarify each thing you have captured previously. Also, you need to decide what you will do with each item. What are your reasons for doing it?

When you know your reasons, you:

- You become aware of the reality and focus on the essential things rather than being carried away by what's urgent. Thus, your anxiety levels are at the barest minimum
- Are in full control because you know what to do and when to do it
- Experience a feeling of relief each time you make a decision. Also, you are not under any intense pressure since you have a clearer perspective about your goals
- Have higher self-esteem since you are responsible for your actions

- Are more productive since you have a reinforced ability to get things done.

3. Update your system regularly

"You have train yourself to see the forest and the tree before your knowledge can be productive" - Peter F. Drucker

You need to review your system regularly to make it useful. Reflect on the essential things in your life, work, current projects, and next actions frequently. Here are a few crucial reasons why you need to review your system regularly:

- A complete review reveals what you are not doing that you should be doing
- Since each action has a clearly defined step, missing one step would affect your result.

Essential Rules for Successful Time Management

It is an open secret that effective time management has loads of benefits. How many times have you heard that better time management reduces stress, saves time, and boosts efficiency? I am sure it's more than you can count. But the truth is, we often struggle to practice effective time management

We procrastinate, then, when we realize that the deadline is close, we start rushing to meet with the timeline. No one has the power to slow downtime, but you can get the most of your day by managing your time correctly.

Here are some proven time management tips to become a master of time management:

1. Batch them together

Batch related work together. For example, schedule a specific period to answer your emails and phone calls. Don't handle these tasks or similar tasks throughout the day. Different projects require a different thought process. Hence, batching together related tasks prevents your brain from switching to different thought processes each time you have to accomplish a different job. Batching helps your mind to eliminate the time it takes for your brain to reorient to accommodate the different new task.

2. Focus on the important aspects

This tip is a credit to Leo Babauta of the Zen Habits blog. According to him, you have to spend a few minutes to understand what needs to be done then, focus on those crucial things alone. Thus, you make every action count and create more value. In this case, less is not more; less is better.

3. Telecommute

Based on research, the average American commutes for at least 25 minutes. It is even predicted that this average time will increase in the nearest future. Add this time to the time it takes you to be prepared for your commute. Then, you will discover that you are wasting considerable time going to and coming back from work. The solution: if it's remotely possible with your job, try telecommuting at least once per week. You will save several hours per week which you can use for other productive means.

4. Make the best of your wait time

By all standards, I'm a patient person. But I can't stand waiting knowing I can spend that time more productively. Hence, I think of the best ways to spend that time. For example, if I'm waiting to see my doctor, I could create a blueprint for an upcoming blog post, listen to a podcast, or read an inspirational book.

5. Incorporate support habits

Charles Duhigg wrote a book called *The Power of Habits*, where he defined keystone habits. These life-transforming habits include meditating, developing daily routines, tracking what you eat, and exercising. By incorporating these support habits into your daily routine, you will replace bad habits with good habits over time. Consequently, you are more focused, healthier, and a better manager of your time.

6. Don't be afraid to say "No."

While you don't want your colleagues to be angry with you, you have limited time just like everyone else. For example, if you don't have spare time, you shouldn't try helping your colleagues with their assigned tasks.

7. Maximize the use of Google Calendar

Though calendars have been a fundamental time management tool for a long time, online calendars have taken it to the next level. You can access an online calendar from multiple devices. Then, use that tool to schedule recurring events, create time blocks, set up reminders, easily schedule meetings, and appointments.

While I think Google Calendar is the best because it's the one I use, Apple Calendar and Outlook can serve the same purpose.

8. Schedule buffer time between tasks or meetings

It may seem like a good use of your time to jump to a new project immediately after completing a previous task. But it has an opposite effect; it clutters your mind. The human brain can only focus for at least 90 minutes at once.

Hence, you need time even if it's a few minutes to recharge your mind, refresh your body, and boost your brain. Walking and meditation are two proven ways to clear your mind and recharge. Otherwise, you will struggle to focus or stay motivated. Based on my experience, a buffer time of 25 minutes between tasks is always ideal.

9. Alter your schedule

Altering your schedule can be a simple and effective solution to your time management struggles. For example, you can wake one hour earlier than your usual time. You can use this extra hour to work on side projects, check your emails, plan your day, exercise, or a combination of these tasks. Also, consider cutting down the amount of TV you watch and maintain the same wake-up routines during weekends.

10. Stop half-work.

According to James Clear, author of the *New York Times* best-seller *Atomic Habits*: "In this age of constant distraction, it's easy to split our focus between societal demands and what we should do. Typically, we are trying to accomplish a task and at the same time checking our to-do lists, emails, and messages. Hence, we can't fully focus on the project we are trying to accomplish."

Here some of the examples he gave of what he called "half-work":

- Your mind is wandering to your email inbox while communicating on the phone
- Writing a report, then, stopping to check your phone for no reason
- Altering your workout routine because you watched a couple of YouTube videos

The point is, when you engage in half-work, it takes you twice the time to accomplish a task, and you will only achieve half the mission. Clear opined that the best solution to half-work is to focus on one project and complete it before thinking about or starting any other task.

For example, pick an exercise and focus on it alone for your workouts. Also, leave your phone in a separate room and devote a significant amount of time on a substantial project. Clear claims that "the best way to achieve deep, focused work and avoid half-work is to eliminate distractions."

11. List all measurable steps to complete a task

All goals and projects are a sum of small moving parts. Hence, you need to clearly define the small moving parts to accomplish a project or goal. A side benefit is that you are motivated by what you have achieved. Thus, you can become focused on what you're yet to accomplish.

When you experience interruptions, ensure you are not entirely carried away by the distraction. A proven way to avoid getting taken away by a distraction is to limit the number of tasks you are performing at a specific time.

12. Apply the Eisenhower principle

You need to identify the urgent and essential tasks from your to-do list before working on them. This concept was first coined by Dwight D. Eisenhower, the 34th US president.

- You achieve personal goals with important tasks
- You achieve immediate goals with urgent tasks. Typically, urgent tasks have immediate consequences but are associated with accomplishing another person's intent.

Eisenhower's principle suggests prioritizing tasks into four groups:

- Not urgent and not important: These are complete distractions. Avoid them.
- Urgent but not important: these are barriers to your tasks, and your co-workers mostly provide them. They seek your help to accomplish their tasks. When this happens, you can suggest another competent person for them or say "No."
- Not urgent but important: These are tasks necessary to accomplish your goals. Thus, ensure you properly prepare for them.
- Urgent and important: These are the first tasks you should undertake every day. Some might be last-minute tasks, while others might be emergency tasks. With proper planning, you can prevent last-minute tasks. But you can't plan for emergency issues. Your best option is to allow a buffer time to deal with such problems. Including time slots for emergencies is one of the best ways to prioritize your tasks.

13. Apply the concept of leverage to complete your task

The smart use of leverage will help you to achieve the most significant returns with the least effort. Use the Pomodoro technique to avoid working overtime. This technique suggests that you "divide and structure your work into 25-minute sessions and a 5-minute break between the sessions."

For example, assuming you're working on a presentation and you've estimated that you need about 150 minutes to accomplish the task. Divide the task into six 25-minute sessions and a 5-minute break between them. Ensure that your sessions are not in conflict with other commitments or plans. Start working once the timer sets off after 25 minutes. Rest for 5 minutes after each session, then, repeat till you complete the sessions. Rest for 30 minutes after completing all the sessions.

14. Track your time

I have saved the best for the last. The first step to proper time management is to determine how you spend your time. You may believe you spend just 25 minutes on emails, while in reality, you spend more than 45 minutes on it per day.

Time apps such as my app calendar, Toggl, or RescueTime offers an easy way for you to track your time and activities weekly. Track your activities for next week, then, use the report to identify your time stealers and make appropriate adjustments.

5 Lesser-Known Productivity Hacks You Need to Know

As a live, breathing human being, there are times you will struggle with your productivity. Often, our inability to produce results consistently and repeatedly is one major thing that holds us back in life. For most of us, there are times we have peak productivity, but most times we have valley productivity. These are the main barriers to our life goals.

Before you can make significant progress in life, you must be productive consistently and repeatedly. You can't have five days of valley productivity and two days of high productivity in any given week. At the very least, you should have five days of high productivity and two days of valley productivity in any given week. However, we all struggle to be highly productive at all times.

Sometimes, we are on high productivity alert. At other times, something zaps our spirit, and our productivity declines. We either indulge in one of our preferred pleasures, or we hit one of life's stumbling blocks. Consequently, our relationships, health, careers, and finances suffer.

What's the solution?

First, you need to identify the impediments to your productivity. Examples of such obstacles include the inability to focus, lack of focus, poor time management skills, and procrastination. If you desire any significant, positive changes in your life, you must learn how to overcome these impediments consistently.

What are productivity hacks?

Hacks are tricks, skills, or shortcuts that can improve your productivity. Bear in mind there are no new productivity hacks; there are only multiple workarounds for us to get and stay productive.

Here are the best five of such hacks:

1. Focus on small and fast wins

Trying to do many things all at once is a common mistake. Another usual error is taking on a huge project in one go. If you want to get things done, start by taking baby steps one at a time.

Split your most important goal into:

- Daily goals
- Weekly goals
- Monthly goals
- Quarterly goals
- Yearly goals

Then, always ask yourself: "What's that one step I will take today that will make me closer to my end goal?" Focus on small and fast wins; avoid dreaming about your big goal.

These small and fast wins will help you to achieve your big goal over time.

Example; big goal: Become a self-published author.

Since a typical book has about 300 pages, you need to a little over 75,000 words (an average of 250 words per page) for the 300 pages.

Breakdown: make it a habit to write 400 words per day rather than thinking about the end goal (75,000 words). Start with 100 words today, and by the end of next week, you must have written another 1,000 words. If you continue that way, you should complete your 300-page book within six months.

That's the magic that happens when you focus on small and fast wins.

2. Don't break the consistency

If you are trying to build a habit within 21 days because you read it or watched it somewhere, you are wrong. The truth is, it takes between 18 and 254 days to build a habit. The key to forming any pattern is consistency. A strong start but giving up too soon is one primary reason why most people are unable to build life-changing habits. If you fall into this category, then, apply the Jerry Seinfeld productivity hack. It's also known as the "don't break the chain" hack.

Here's an excerpt from an article on life hacker by Brad Isaac in which Jerry Seinfeld explains this hack:

"The best way to be the best comic is to create better jokes. Writing every day is the way to create better jokes. Use a unique calendar system as a leverage technique to pressure yourself to write. Get a wall calendar with a whole year on one page and hang it where it can be prominent. Then, use a big red magic marker to put a big red x over each day you perform your task. You should have a chain after a few days of consistent practice. The chain will keep growing, provided you keep at it. After a few weeks of consistency, you will be motivated to keep the chain growing. Thus, your only task is to avoid breaking the chain."

This hack is useful because it helps you to be consistent with your skill or talent.

The three steps to get started with this hack:

Step 1: Figure out your skill or learn it. You can choose to become a master at SEO, a highly sought-after programmer or an exceptional stand-up comedian. This is a vital step; don't skip it.

Step 2: Put up a one-year calendar on a prominent space in your home, office, or workplace.

Step 3: As you devote time to work on that skill, cross each day with a big x. Focus on lengthening the chain. Your only task is to avoid breaking the chain.

3. Use a standing desk

I know it seems crazy, but using a standing desk can improve your focus and productivity by up to 46%. New evidence by Texas A & M University research suggests that employees using standing desks are 46% more productive than those using the traditional seated desk configurations. Now, most hip office use standing desks. Also, FF Venture capital discovered that results in more active sharing of ideas. It is a well-known fact Thomas Jefferson, and a few other prominent individuals worked at standing desks for most days of their lives.

Other benefits of working at a standing desk at home or workplace include:

- Increased productivity. You won't check your inbox too frequently
- Calorie reduction. Using a standing desk exercises the significant muscles in your legs
- Improved focus. It is normal to feel a sense of urgency when standing. Thus, you are more focused and can complete tasks on time
- Improvements to your digestive health. A standing desk prevents you from sleeping at your desk. Thus, you experience less fatigue.

When you use standing desks, you have little or no urge to multitask, switch between websites, check email, and be distracted in any other way.

How to get started:
- **Start in small cycles.** Rather than start working at your standing desk for straight hours. Start with baby steps. Start with 20 minutes per day, then increase this time gradually till you can ultimately spend your day on a standing desk
- **Use Pinterest** or similar sites to get creative ideas on setting up your standing desk
- **Take breaks.** Avoid stiffness or fatigue by consuming a cup of coffee, practicing squats or going for a short walk.

4. Implement the 2-minute rule

It is surprising to know that you can accomplish quite a lot within two minutes. The inclusion of mundane tasks in a daily to-do list is one of the reasons why 90% of people never achieve the tasks on their to-do lists. Thus, you need a systemic approach to tackling your to-do list. That systemic approach is the 2-minute rule.

By implementing the 2-minute rule, you focus on essential tasks and eliminate the unimportant tasks.

The 2-minute rule is split into two parts:

- Start and complete anything that can be accomplished within two minutes
- Start anything that takes more than two minutes to accomplish

Part 1. Start and complete anything that can be accomplished within two minutes

Don't add this 2-minute task to your to-do list, don't procrastinate about it and don't outsource it. Do it immediately and forget about it. Tasks that fit into a 2-minute project include cleaning up clutter, sending that email, taking out the garbage, tossing the laundry in the washing machine, washing your dishes immediately after your meal.

With time, you will start uncovering more 2-minute tasks. Build and maintain excitement in your workday by ticking off this 2-minute task. There's a sense of accomplishment synonymous with getting things done. By micro-managing unimportant tasks through the 2-minute principle, you can manage your daily to-do lists with greater effectiveness.

Part 2. Start anything that takes more than two minutes to accomplish

If you have 2-hour, 2-day, 2-week, or 2-month tasks, then, you may start wondering how to accomplish them down within two minutes. When you build momentum by accomplishing a 2-minute task, you feel better equipped to perform more significant tasks. This is one primary reason why the 2-minute rule is quite potent.

Examples of tasks you can turn into a 2-minutes project include:

- "Run three miles," is now "Tie my running shoes."
- "Fold the laundry" becomes "Fold one pair of socks."
- "Study for class" turns to "Open my notes."
- "Do 20 minutes of yoga" starts with "Take out my yoga mat."
- "Read before bed each night" becomes "Read one page."

You set the precedence to move onto more significant tasks by using the 2-minute rule to take immediate action on your goals.

5. Miscellaneous hacks
1. When browsing with Google Chrome
- **Pin websites to desktop**

If you visit some websites regularly, pin them to your desktop as apps. To do this, open the website you want to pin, go to Chrome settings, more tools, then, click on "create shortcut."

- **Use these popular Chrome shortcuts**
    - Ctrl+shift+n: opening a new window in incognito mode
    - Ctrl+j: open "recent downloads"
    - Shift+esc: Opens Google Chrome's task manager

- Alt+enter: open URL in a new tab after typing the URL manually
- Ctrl/shift+f5: reload the current page while ignoring cached content

2. *Do this last thing each night but the first thing each morning*

Send yourself an email before you sleep. This email should contain your top three goals for the next day. This is an often-overlooked productivity hack, yet it is straightforward.

Most times, you may have forgotten what you even wrote, probably because of stress, exhaustion, or a good night's sleep.

Chapter 3 - A Guide to Goal-Setting

All About the Goal-Setting Theory of Motivation

Edwin Locke proposed the goal-setting theory of motivation in the 1960s. This theory states that goal setting hugely depends on task performance. It says that specific, challenging goals with appropriate feedback results in higher and better task performance.

Goals indicate and guide the employee on the task to be achieved and the number of efforts required to accomplish it.

The efficiency of the goal depends on the type and quality of the goal.

Imagine you are 40 pounds overweight and need to drop the extra weight. Here are some options you have when setting the goal:

- "I want to shed the extra pounds before this time next year. I will review my diet and make appropriate recommendations." This goal isn't specific and lacks clarity. You need to specify the amount of weight you want to lose within that period and the particular steps to shedding this extra weight.
- "I will lose two pounds a week over the next four months. My exercise routine will be 40 minutes per day, five days a week. Also, I will include whole-grain products, vegetables, and three fruit servings in my diet. Lastly, I won't eat out at all for the next month. Then, I will only eat out once per week after the next month." This is a more

specific and more clearly-defined goal than the previous one.

The principal motivation is the willingness to work towards achieving the set goal. Easy, general, and vague goals are less motivating than clear, specific, and challenging goals.

Goal-Setting Principles

Based on his research in 1968, Dr. Edwin Locke published an article titled, *'Towards a theory of task motivation and incentives."* In this article, he provided proof that a clearly-defined goal with proper feedback motivates people to accomplish their goals. He also opined that the thrills involved in achieving a goal is a motivation in itself and improves performance. Summarily, Locke suggests that we tend to work harder to attain specific and challenging goals, especially in a work environment.

Years later, Dr. Gary Latham conducted his goal setting research in a work environment. Like Locke, he aimed to establish the correlation between setting goals and employee performance in the workplace.

In 1990, Locke and Latham jointly published their most famous work, *"A theory of goal setting & task performance."* The published work emphasized the importance of setting a specific and challenging goal. They also developed five basic principles responsible for success in goal setting.

Goals should:

- Be clear. A clearly-defined goal is more achievable than a poorly-defined one. Goals with a specific timeline of completion are usually the most effective.
- Be challenging. A goal with a slight level of difficulty will provide you with the motivation to accomplish the goal

- Involve a level of commitment. When you are committed to your goal, you will make the necessary effort to achieve the goal. Also, being accountable can increase your level of commitment towards the goal. One simple and effective way to be responsible is to share your goal with a friend, relative, or trusted colleague.
- Have appropriate feedback. However, there has to be proper feedback to improve performance towards achieving the next goal. Feedback is the tool to regulate goal difficulties, make clarifications, and gain reputation. In a work environment, feedback helps the employee to be more involved in attaining the next goal. Hence, they become more satisfied with their job.
- Include the time for overcoming the learning curve. This is especially true for complex projects. Thus, having the time to master the learning curve gives you the best chance of success.

When employees are involved in setting the goal, they are more receptive towards the goal and are more involved in attaining the goal.

The goal-setting theory makes two specific assumptions:

Assumption #1: Goal Commitment

The goal-setting theory assumes that the individual will not abandon the goal because he's fully committed to it. However, you can only be committed to a goal when:

- It is open, accessible and the widespread
- You are not assigned the goal, but you are the one setting the goal
- Your set goal is consistent with your corporation; s goals and vision

Assumption #2: Self-Efficiency

This is your self-confidence and faith in performing the task. Your level of self-efficiency will determine the amount of effort you will apply when struggling with any aspect of the project. The reverse is also true; if your level of self-efficiency becomes too low, you may even quit before accomplishing the task.

How to Apply the Goal-Setting Theory in Your Life

Carefully consider the goals you set when trying to improve an aspect of your daily life. Ensure that each task obeys the goal-setting principles discussed above.

Ensure you set goals that are suitable to one's abilities. For example, you could help your child succeed academically by allowing her to set the goal. For example, assume she wants to get 100% in her next English test. Not only is she committed to this goal, but the goal is also clear and challenging.

Now, you only need to discuss whether or not the goal is attainable. If she typically gets Cs in English assignments, it might be a poor goal to achieve a perfect score at the next attempt. Then, you need to develop specific steps towards achieving the goal. You also need to consider the amount of time required to achieve the objective and the complexity involved.

Ultimately, her goal might be: "I want a 100% score in my English test. I will start practicing neat and clean handwriting, then, learn how to use the appropriate words. My dad will give me feedback on how to fix my mistakes." Now, this is a specific plan to receive proper feedback because it is a clear, achievable goal, and she has the right motivation to achieve it. According to the goal-setting theory, she will perform better in her next test even if she couldn't obtain 100% on it.

The only limitation to the goal-setting theory is that it can fail when you lack the skill and competence to perform necessary actions towards achieving the goal.

Bear these principles in mind when next you want to determine your (individual or team) goals:

1. Set clear and precise goals

A clear goal is measurable and is devoid of understanding. The desired outcome will determine the explicitness of the objective and how it will be measured. Synonymous with the SMART goal-setting principle, clear goals should improve the understanding of the task, make results measurable and success inevitable. Consider how you will measure results. Does your goal excite you? Is it challenging enough? As you think about it, do you feel the motivation to complete it? If you answered negatively to any of these questions, you might have to reconsider this goal.

Clear goal:

- Implement technology to reduce product development time from 20 minutes to 15 minutes by the end of the year
- I want to lose 15 pounds in 2 months

Unclear goal:

- Decrease product development time
- I want to lose weight

When your goal is concrete and measurable, achieving it becomes easily possible, and you can easily track your progress.

2. Make your goals challenging

"A goal that inspires your hopes, liberates your energy and commands your thoughts will make you happy." - Andrew Carnegie.

To ensure you have the right degree of challenge, setting challenging goals requires a considerable balance. Your motivation and performance depend on the simplicity or difficulty in achieving the goal. You reach the highest level of motivation when your goal lies between difficult and easy.

The next time you set goals, make sure they are trying but attainable, challenging, but realistic. Here are a few questions you can ask yourself when setting your goals:

- Are they realistic and achievable?
- Do they provide enough motivation?
- Do they give enough challenge?

Challenging:

- Convert 65% more prospects to clients in Q3 FY 2018-19 compared with 45% Q2 FY 2018-19.
- Lose 40 pounds within two months

Easily achievable:

- Convert 1% more prospects to clients in Q3 FY 2018-19 compared to Q2 FY 2018-19.
- Lose 1 pound within two months

Your goal should be difficult enough to make you feel accomplished.

3. *Truly and genuinely commit to your goals*

You must fully understand and agree to your goals, whether you are setting the goal for yourself, your employees, or teammates before you can accomplish such goals. Mostly, when working in a team, your teammates will more likely work harder for the objective provided they have been involved in setting the goal.

You shouldn't have any motivation problem till the goal is accomplished, provided the goal is achievable and consistent with the aspirations of all your teammates.

Imagine the tasks you accomplish daily at work; which ones do you exert the most effort and which ones do you perform without interest or enthusiasm. Your motivation to achieve your goals depends on your emotional commitment to the objective.

Correct: Project manager and his team decide the expected outcome of a meeting subject to each teammate's talent and skills.

Incorrect: Project manager does not consider his team's bandwidth and capabilities before assigning goals to each of them.

4. Obtain feedback on your progress

"Goal setting becomes hugely effective when you have feedback that shows progress relative to the intended goal" - Prof. Edwin Locke

Once you've chosen the right goal, you should obtain feedback to determine your level of progress. Thus, you can decide whether to adjust the goal or adjust your approach to attain the goal. Feedback can be self-adjudged, but it usually comes from other people.

Correct:

- Perform weekly checks on the design department to monitor their progress. Provide feedback on whether they need to alter the process, or they are on track.
- Tweak weight loss routine after losing one pound in two weeks

Incorrect:

- Set and forget about a task. When the deadline approaches, start getting anxious about completing the task.
- Wait after two months before tracking any changes

Frequently set aside some time to review your goals and track your progress. Thus, you are motivated continuously through the process of achieving your goal.

5. *Simplify complex tasks*

Be careful not to complicate your goals. When your objectives become too complicated, it negatively affects your motivation, productivity, and morale. Most people become overwhelmed when goals become highly complex. When you have complex goals, allow enough time to learn (when necessary), practice and improve performance until the goal is achieved. When necessary, modify the goal by reassessing its complexity or difficulty. You can also break those goals into smaller sub-goals.

Bear in mind that nothing worth its salt will ever be easily accomplished. But using simpler, less-complicated sub-tasks can help you to break down and overcome daunting tasks.

Remember that *"the journey of a thousand miles starts with taking the first step"* - Lao Tzu

Correct: Break down and distribute target sales among all salespeople, depending on their abilities. Thus, the entire target sales can be achieved within a specific period.

Incorrect: Expect one salesperson to achieve the entire target sales within a specific period

You need to keep working at your goal setting, just like every other aspect of your life. Use the principles to implement your life goals, and you will be surprised at the greatness you will achieve.

15 of the Best Tips for Effective Goal-Setting

You're virtually guaranteed success when you are clear about your life's purpose. You can determine your vision, convert your desires into achievable goals, and act on them.

My past experiences have taught me that being selective about my new year's goals, and thinking of ways to accomplish them has been hugely helpful. Goal setting is one proven way to transform impressive resolutions into actual results. Research shows that we are more likely to achieve our goals provided they are measurable.

When you have finished reading this section, you should have proven tips you can use to set your goals with greater efficiency:

1. **Make it physical.** Write down or type out your goals and action plans on paper. As you write them down, you will be more inclined to flesh them out. Thus, your action plans will not just be an outline. It will be a detailed roadmap you can follow.
2. **Regular review is key.** You should ensure that you review your goals at least once in a month, if not once a week. You can schedule an appointment with yourself, a team member, a trusted colleague, or relative for the review. Hence, you can track your level of progress easily. I review my yearly goals every week to ensure I'm on the right track of progress towards my goal.
3. **Challenge yourself without being stupid.** While it is good to choose goals that will excite and stretch you, you

must also ensure that these goals are attainable. Thus, you can truly measure your progress over a specific period. The idea is to accomplish the goals and have something valuable you can celebrate at the end of the year. If you constantly have unachievable goals or white elephant projects, you start developing a habit of failure.

4. **Be exact with your action plans.** Write down the exact steps that can help you to accomplish your goal. For example, you need to show your business plan to potential investors when starting a business before they can take you seriously.
5. **Quality is always better than quantity.** Rather than having a long wish list of tasks which you may never accomplish, why not have three or four solid goals? Once you've accomplished the most important goals, you can add more goals later.
6. **Be specific.** For example: create a blog with 10,000 monthly visitors is more specific than creating a blog with thousands of monthly visitors. Similarly, "gaining 1,500 Twitter followers" is more specific than "having a strong social media presence."
7. **Deadlines make concrete goals.** Your action plan is incomplete without a timeline to achieve the goal. Break down your big goal to smaller sub-goals. Then, set deadlines for these sub-goals till you attain the big goal.
8. **Accountability is important.** Share your goals with a friend or a loved one. They will make you accountable for achieving your goal. The law of commitment states that "When we tell others what we intend to accomplish, we have a natural tendency to remain committed till we achieve it." Thus, you have the needed impetus to take all the necessary steps until you can attain your goal.

9. **Make it obvious.** Tape your goals where they are pronounced. This place can be your door fridge or your bathroom mirror. If you stick it in a drawer, you will forget about it, and it won't do you any good. The idea here is to maintain top of mind awareness. You will easily forget what's not on top of your mind. Another way to keep your goals top of mind is to read your goals every day.
10. **Maintain flexibility.** When you have to scale back, recalibrate, or revise to take care of emergencies, ensure that these changes move you forward. This is one benefit of having a monthly review of your yearly goals.
11. **Love and appreciate the process.** The results you desire and the goal-setting process to achieve the goal are equally important. If you constantly think about what you're yet to achieve, you won't appreciate the process or the sub-goals you've already achieved. When you appreciate and honor the adventure, you will remain positive, confident, and motivated.
12. **Use the rule of 5.** The rule of 5 ensures that you take daily steps towards attaining your goals. Identify and accomplish five specific steps that will get you closer to your goal. These steps don't have to be big. Sending an email or making a quick call is fine provided they are relevant to your goal. But quit for the day until you complete these five steps. Thus, you have a proven structure to maximize your day and give you a clarity of what you can achieve daily. If you use this rule and stick with it, you can make consistent progress without exhausting yourself. Where necessary, you can scale back your goals or round them up.
13. **Don't neglect self-care.** If you're malnourished, overworked, or stressed, you may never attain your goals.

If you do, you may suffer ill-health as a result of the stress and overwork. While achieving your dreams, don't neglect self-care. Your body will thank you, and you will preserve your health and sanity.

14. **Keep score.** Why do you check the score immediately you tune into a sports station? You want to know which team is winning and how long for them to hold on. You should also be keeping score with the goals you've set. I suggest you use a physical chart. Identify the goal and outline the steps you need to achieve this goal. Track your progress and for every success, reward yourself. Using visual charts will show you that you are avoiding any shortcuts.
15. **Never give up.** If you don't give up but implement the tips above, you will succeed and achieve your goals even faster.

8 Common Reasons Why To-Do Lists Fail

Most people using to-do lists struggle to cross-out every item on the list by the time they are off to bed in the night. Even the tasks completed aren't part of the to-do lists. If to-do lists don't work for you, they would seem to be highly ineffective. You may be killing your productivity with your to-do lists. This section reveals why your to-do lists fail and what you can do about it.

1. You're allowing energy vampires

These are self-centered people who sap your energy without considering your time and priorities. They are the ones continually seeking your help over one task or the other. Most times, these are time-consuming tasks that are neither beneficial to you or on your to-do list.

If the energy vampire is a work colleague, you can send him this simple message. "I'm under a tight deadline now, and unfortunately, I can't help out at the moment." If this colleague remains persistent, send him a message similar to the one below: "I'm currently working on [state your current task here]. But I can loop in my supervisor and ask him how to prioritize."

2. You're writing your to-do list in the morning

Write your to-do list before going to bed. Thus, you avoid wasting your energized morning mojo to develop your daily tasks. A side benefit of creating your to-do list before going to bed is that it calms your mind. Psychiatrists and psychologists even recommend this technique to avoid anxiety. Keep out unwanted thoughts by establishing a plan for your next 24-hours. You won't disturb your sleep with thoughts of "you have a parent meeting at 2 pm" or "you must finish the report by 6 pm tomorrow."

3. Your to-do list has too many items

Out of 6,500 LinkedIn professionals, only 11% of them finish their to-do tasks by the end of the day. When you have too many items on your to-do list, you are setting yourself up for failure. Also, you deprive yourself of that end-of-day excitement of accomplishing your daily task. Also, when your to-do list is too much, it becomes highly discouraging. You will be more inclined to procrastinate since you won't know where to start.

Choosing at most three most important tasks is one effective way I've found to improve my productivity and manage my time correctly. Your most important tasks are measurable, generative, have meaning when completed, and move you towards accomplishing your goals.

4. You don't create time for urgent distractions

After making all the efforts to understand and write down your priorities. An email from a co-worker or a piece of breaking news is all it takes to distract you. So, you're off track the moment you receive your first urgent message despite all your productivity efforts.

A simple and effective solution is to create space in your schedule without any task. Thus, you have space to accommodate emergencies. Then, on days where there are no emergencies, you finish your day early and take the rest of the day off. You can also take proactive measures to avoid distractions. Adjust your email settings only to receive messages from specific people, set your phone calls to voicemails and make your status "busy" on private chats.

5. Your to-do list lack specificity

In an interview with Bloomberg Business, David Allen said, "Ninety-nine percent of every to-do list I have seen is an incomplete list of unclear stuff. You will see things like 'bank,' 'doctor,' or 'mom.' While these may look good, you need to include an action step with it." Instead of 'bank,' write down the specific task such as 'create a new savings account at the bank'."

6. You're not sorting your to-do list

After identifying your three most important tasks for the day, classify other goals into:

- A long-term list
- A weekly list.

Your long-term list should contain your 3-month or 6-month goal. For example, "completely cut out all unnecessary expenses." the weekly to-do list for this 6-month goal would be: "Stop eating out for the next X weeks."

7. Your to-do list lacks a deadline

There is no difference between a wish list and a to-do list without deadlines. Deadlines tilt us towards taking action. Where there are no deadlines, you lack the motivation to take action. This is one reason why your to-do list keeps growing without finishing most of the tasks on the list.

When you set deadlines, you prioritize tasks or projects to complete them within a specified timeframe. Remember Parkinson's law: *"Work expands to fill the time available for its completion."* You need to assign deadlines to your to-do items. Otherwise, don't be surprised that you can't finish most of the tasks.

8. You don't understand why you need a to-do list

For most people, when you ask them the basis for creating a to-do list, their answer is always: "to get things done." However, that's the wrong reason for creating a properly-designed to-do list. The primary purpose of a to-do list is to organize and highlight your most important tasks. By writing them down, you gain a panoramic view of your most essential duties.

A properly-designed to-do list should help you concentrate on the right work and avoid any distractions. Your task list is a tool to get the right things done; it's not a tool to get everything done. Reread the statement above again until you correctly understand the difference. When you misunderstand the role of your to-do list, you will create and use an ineffective one. Thus, rather than increase your productivity, you end up restricting it.

Now you have a to-do list approach that can make your day rather than break it. Note that you should write this long-term and weekly to-do list on a separate page in your journal.

Chapter 4 - The Secrets of Productivity

How to Prioritize When Everything Is Important

You're not alone; we all don't enough time to do everything we want to do. However, does everything on your to-do list feel important (or your superior feels that way)? Then, it's time for you to implement any of the prioritization techniques in this section. Thus, your to-do list can become more manageable and conquerable.

What's a Prioritization Technique?

Which of the 150 tasks on your task list is the most important? The prioritization technique will help you to answer this question correctly. This technique provides you with a formal method to evaluate the importance of finishing each task on your list. By implementing the prioritization process, you can make the right decisions about the project you need to do. But delete the ones that are less urgent and less important. You can even specify a period for a particular task.

The prioritization techniques solve two vital issues:

Issue #1: Do you feel you've spent all your day performing urgent tasks for everyone who've sought your help? Then, a prioritized list will help you to avoid unreasonable last-minute panic assignments and regain control of your time.

Issue #2: Are those meeting requests or incoming emails that important? You'll never complete important work when you allow other people to create your to-do list for you through incoming emails and meeting requests. When you know the specific tasks to focus on and the reason to focus on that task, you can easily justify delaying answering that email or declining a meeting invite.

During my time in a product development team, we often use our prioritized list to prevent distractions and delays. When stakeholders made new and urgent requests, we show them the prioritized list. Then, ask, "Which task should we remove to accommodate your new request?" Often, once they see the importance of the other items on the list, their urgent requests suddenly become less urgent.

You can also use this technique to manage priorities with your family, co-workers, and your boss. It can also work for that part of your brain that's always searching for new ideas, giving you reasons to procrastinate on valuable work.

Use these prioritization techniques to focus on your most important work. You have to choose the right prioritization technique that makes sense and works for you. Fortunately, you can find a method that works for you from any of these prioritization techniques:

1. Priority Matrix

This technique involves distributing your tasks into a 4-box array. The y-axis represents a value, while the x-axis represents another one. Then, each quadrant represents a priority defined by the values.

The image below illustrated this technique.

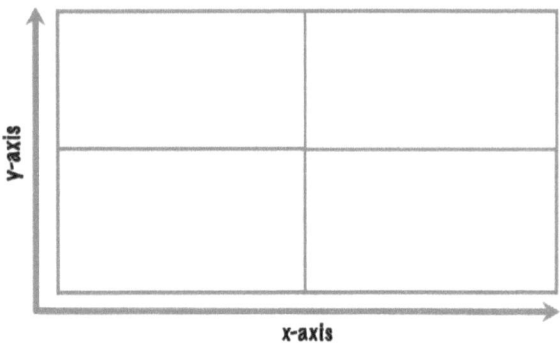

The Eisenhower matrix is a famous example of a priority matrix. In this matrix, urgency is the x-axis value, while importance is the y-axis value. Use urgency and importance to evaluate tasks, before placing each task in the correct quadrant. Thus, the Eisenhower matrix looks like the image below:

	Importance	
	Important, but not urgent	Important and Urgent
	Not urgent or important	Urgent, but not important

Urgency

After placing each task in its suitable quadrant, you can determine what you need to delete from your list. You can also uncover what you need to delegate, what you need to work on later, and what you need to work on now.

Note that you can use any values that make sense to you as your x-and y-axis values in the priority matrix.

Here are two additional examples:

a. Effort-impact matrix

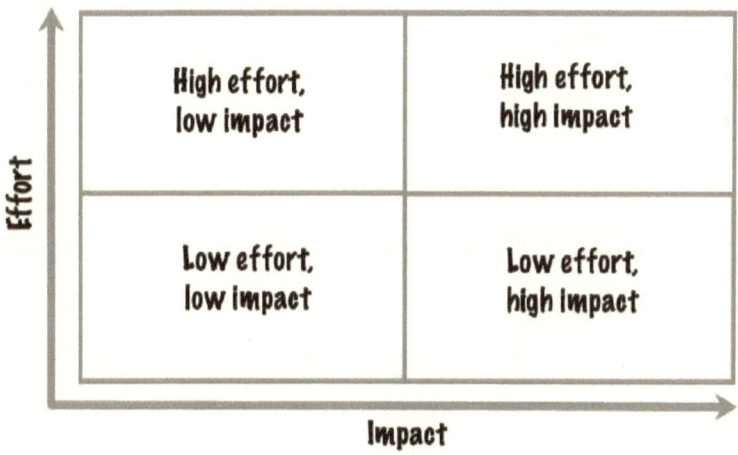

In this matrix, you assess tasks based on the effort you will exert to complete them and the impact of completing them. Your priorities are the tasks in the two right-side quadrants. Since the "low effort, high impact" tasks represent quick wins; they are likely your highest priorities.

b. Value-cost matrix

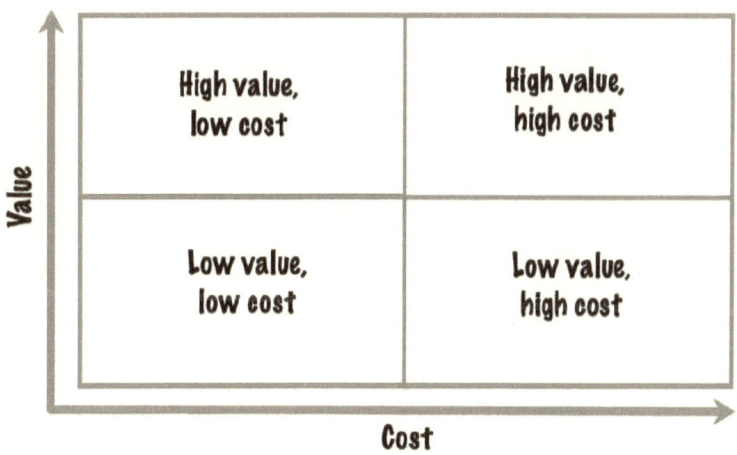

In this matrix, your priorities are the top two quadrants. Your quick wins are the "high value, low cost" tasks, but you should avoid executing "low value, high cost" tasks. If the priority matrix resonates with you, you can build your matrices in a spreadsheet, on paper, use the priority matrix app or the free Eisenhower matrix app.

2. MoSCoW (pronounced just like Russia's capital city)

In this simple prioritization technique, you categorize every task on your to-do list into four:

- M tasks-must do: Highly important tasks
- S tasks-should do: Though they are lower of a lower priority than m tasks, the s tasks are things you should do
- C tasks-could do: These are tasks you'd like to do. However, if you don't do them, it won't matter at all
- W tasks-won't do: These are tasks that aren't worth your time at all

How to use this technique

Use the MoSCoW to categorize each task. The order of priority of your tasks should be M, S, and C. Delete your W tasks.

Then, start working on your list from the top-down, and you can be sure that you're working on your highest-priority tasks.

Trello or any other Kanban app (available on Android and iTunes stores) is very useful for the MoSCoW method. Specify the order of each task by dragging and dropping them within the lists.

For optimal results with the MoSCoW method, ensure you add all your tasks to a master list before categorizing them. Use a zap (an automated Zapier workflow) to make this addition; it automates the movement of your mini-projects from Slack and your email inbox to your master to-do list.

3. ABCDE

A major demerit of the MoSCoW technique is that you can't use it for task delegation. The best alternative is to use Brian Tracy's ABCDE method (details in his "Eat The Frog" book). The ABCDE method is similar to the MoSCoW method.

- The A tasks are the M tasks in the MoSCoW method - do them
- The B tasks are the s tasks in the MoSCoW method
- The C tasks are the c tasks in the MoSCoW method
- The D tasks are tasks you should automate or delegate - this is the difference
- The E tasks are the w tasks in the MoSCoW method - delete them

Use the priority of each project to assign a letter to it. By delegating the D tasks and removing the E tasks, you can focus on the A, B, and C tasks - the most critical tasks.

You can also use Kanban apps for this technique. Your master list should sub-lists with A, B, C, D, and E tasks. Drag and drop tasks into the right category from the master list, then, start with your A tasks.

4. Agile Prioritization

This prioritization method, also known as scrum prioritization, relies on ordering your tasks. If you have 15 to-dos on your task list, use priority and sequence to arrange the mini-projects from 1-15. Scrum prioritization is highly effective when the series is highly essential. For example, assuming your most important task is to retile your bathroom floor, but they also have to run new pipes. Though running new pipes is a lower priority, it needs to be completed first because it will affect your most important task: retiling the floor.

There are three criteria for evaluating task in scrum prioritization:

- The importance of the project
- The significance of the project relative to other tasks
- Other projects that can affect this task

Assign each of these criteria a number 1 to N (N = total number of items on your list). Every item should have a unique number. No two tasks can be #1. Though scrum prioritization can be combined with the MoSCoW and ABCDE techniques, it's also useful on its own. Consider the inter-dependence of the tasks on one another before categorizing them by priority. Then, arrange them in order of completion.

Any drag-and-drop to-do list app is suitable for scrum prioritization. But for efficiency, rather than using drag and drop tools, you can use Yodiz (a scrum-specific tool) to assign numbers to each task. Yodiz has a free plan.

5. Bubble Sort

Let's rephrase criteria #2 of the scrum prioritization technique to "how important is a task relative to other tasks?" The bubble sort is a technique that compares the importance of tasks relative to one another. Hence, it's a useful technique for answering the question above. The first step to using this technique is to arrange all your to-do items on a horizontal grid:

| Task 1 | Task 2 | Task 3 | Task 4 | Task 5 | Task 6 |

Your next step is to compare the first two tasks and identify the most important one. Then, move the most critical item to the top left. Using the image above, assuming task 2 is more important than item 1, then, it becomes the first task of the horizontal grid.

Continue to compare the two closest tasks until you exhaust the list of tasks using the question above as the basis for rearranging the order of items.

After reordering the list completely, your least important priority is now to the far right, while your most important priority is now on the far left.

An example of a completely reordered list in order of priority is shown below:

| Task 2 | Task 1 | Task 6 | Task 4 | Task 3 | Task 5 |

Though there are no specific tools suitable for this technique, any project management app appropriate for drag-and-drop prioritization can work effectively. But instead of working on tasks from left-to-right, you work on them from top-to-bottom.

6. The 1-3-9 Technique

This technique allows you to prioritize urgent but less important tasks. Each day you are to complete 13 tasks:

- Nine low-importance items
- Three somewhat important tasks
- One crucial task

First, work and complete your one tasks, then, your three tasks and lastly, your nine tasks. The 1-3-9 method helps you to work on the most important of your less important tasks.

7. Two Lists

This technique is credited to Warren Buffet. Here's how it works: write down 25 to-do tasks, then, circle the top five items on this list. Next, group these tasks into two extensive lists. The first list which contains the five tasks you circled is now your to-do list. The second list which includes the other 20 items is now your don't do list. Complete all your five to-do tasks before spending any time on your don't do list. While you could accomplish this technique with any app that allows you to move tasks between lists, it is a technique designed to be performed on paper.

How to Choose Your Most Suitable Prioritization Technique

The goal of these prioritization techniques is the same - to help you work on your highest priority tasks. Hence, it doesn't matter whether you use one technique, multiple techniques, or combine parts of the different techniques. You must ensure that the technique you choose makes sense, feels natural, and is adequate for you.

The Chunking Technique for Making Your Goals Achievable

These days, we are pulled in a lot of directions on our personal and professional lives that the idea of free becomes an illusion. But imagine:

- You can bring higher efficiency to your life
- You can focus on achieving your goals rather than trying to accomplish an infinite number of tasks on your to-do lists

Imagine the free time it will open in your life and the positive change in the quality of your life. This desire to create free time is the basis of the rapid planning method (RPM). Apart from being a time management system, RPM helps you to focus on critical aspects that can help you to organize your life more efficiently. Thus, you can maximize your sense of fulfillment, joy, and optimize your desired outcomes. The assumption is that you are more driven to take actions that lead to your success when you have a clarity of purpose that drives your actions. Chunking (a highly efficient way to maximize your day) is one of the core components of RPM.

What is Chunking?

Chunking means arranging information into bit-sized pieces to produce your desired outcome without shutdown or stress. One source of stress in our lives is that we don't have enough time to do an infinite number of things for our lives. This strong emotion to get things done leads to the creation of to-do lists. But a large number of items on the list can lead to frustration. Thus, we won't even tackle any project on our list.

Based on my experience, three chunking methods have been the most effective:

- Chunk down by quantity
- Chunk down by the time
- Chunk down by actionable steps

1. *Chunk down by quantity*

This means setting a quota. If you are a writer, you can set a quota for your writing. For example, you can write a maximum of 3 pages per day until you complete your novel.

Alternatively, your quota can be a word count. An example is a national novel writing month challenge. If you are a participant, you will be required to write 1,667 words per day, and by the end of the month, you would have completed a 50,000-word book.

Here are three other examples of chunking down a goal by quantity:

- Hit 300 balls daily to improve your tennis
- Learn ten French words per day for 100 days to improve your French fluency
- Do one drawing per day for one year to improve your drawing fluency

2. *Chunk down by the time*

A while back, I was overweight because I was making bad food choices, eating out a lot, and wasn't exercising. After choosing to shed some pounds, my nutritionist and I developed a plan for me to lose 30 pounds in three months. He provided me with a menu of what to eat during this month. I was also instructed to walk one hour daily.

Walking one hour per day became a significant component of chunking down my goal. Thus, I used the time to chunk down my goal of losing weight.

Here are some other goals that can be chunked down by time:

- Declutter for 10 minutes daily to be organized
- Practice piano for 40 minutes daily to become a master pianist
- Meditate for 15 minutes daily to manage stress

However, spending an hour per day to achieve my important goals remains my favorite way of chunking down my goals.

3. Chunk down by actionable steps

By creating a list of actionable steps, you can chunk down a goal you are not sure you could achieve. Goal, sub-goals, and actionable steps are three terms we would use to describe this method.

By definition,

- The goals are the target you intend to achieve
- Sub-goals are the milestones to achieve the goals
- Actionable steps are the single tasks to accomplish each sub-goal

Assuming you intend to "create a video course," but you've never created a course or made videos. Your first step is to establish a deadline for the video course creation. Let's use a 6-month (180-day) deadline. Next, open excel and create 180 spaces (a space for each day); this is your actionable steps list.

Now, create ten sub-goals to achieve your big goal. Anytime you need help with any creating the sub-goals, you can:

- talk to a video course creation expert,
- read a book about it,
- watch some YouTube videos, or perform online research.

For our video course creation example, here are ten sub-goals to achieve this goal:

- Suitable equipment
- Learning how to use the equipment
- Developing the title for the course
- Validate your title idea
- Develop your outline
- Develop the script
- Design the slides

- Start recording the videos
- Edit your videos (I recommend you outsource)
- Launch your course

To make things easy, let's assume each sub-goal has a deadline of 18 days (i.e., 180 days (the total deadline) divided by 10 (the number of sub-goals)). Thus, we need 18 actionable steps to achieve each sub-goal.

You can use the following guideline to create your actionable steps.

Actionable step for each day:

- One - what you can do right away to get started
- Two - the next physical action to take
- Repeat the steps above till you have actionable steps to complete your first sub-goal

If you complete a sub-goal in less 18 days, move to the next sub-goal. Then, continue until you accomplish your goal. As write down actionable steps, ask yourself this question: "Am I capable of taking the step immediately?" If your answer is "yes," then include this actionable step. Otherwise, break down this step further.

You can also use the CRUMBB technique, an acronym for "clearly realizable unit that's a meaningful building block." Realizable means you can take action immediately, while Meaningful means it moves you closer to complete your goal. You can read more about the CRUMBB method in a book titled "master the moment" written by best-selling author, Pat Brans.

Use any of the three methods to chunk down your goals. By breaking down your goals and tackling them in bite-sized pieces, you can easily save time and achieve your goals.

5 of the Biggest Productivity Killers and How to Overcome Them

We all aspire to become good time managers and achieve high levels of productivity. However, we experience several obstacles and distractions hinder us from achieving the goals before we can even think of surpassing such goals.

In this section of the chapter, you will discover severe time-wasters and top productivity killers.

1. Busyness

Activities in this category include calling unnecessary meetings, making unnecessary phone calls, organizing email, and cleaning the desk. Most people indulge in excess busywork for the sake of being busy. When you indulge in these non-substantial activities, you are not productive.

How to overcome: set aside one hour per day to delegate all these tasks. Then, you can easily focus on your high priority list of items.

2. Excessive planning

With planning, you are sure you won't miss any important thing. You already know your next actions, and you can focus on your goals with your task list. However, rather than do any actual work, it's much easier to spend time to update and organize your calendar.

How to overcome: set aside one day in 21 days to review undone tasks. Also, spend 15 minutes each morning to review your previous day's performance and update your goals for the day. Evernote and Day One apps are quite useful for this purpose.

3. Less sleep

One of the biggest productivity killers is sleeping less and staying up late. When you sleep less, you do things slowly because it is tough for you to get moving. Hence, you become addicted to coffee before you can have a productive day.

While it may not be necessary to get a full eight hours of sleep, ensure you get enough sleep that makes you productive for the day. Thus, you avoid relying on chemicals which can pose a severe health issue in the nearest future.

4. Email inbox

Email is highly addictive, and it is the biggest time sucker in business or personal life. Worse, you won't get any work done. When you email a client or colleague, and you discuss work, you are not dealing with your problems but helping others solve their problem.

3 simple and effective ways to overcome email overwhelm:

1. Check your email three times per day. This can be an hour before you get to work, after lunch, and just before you sleep. Thus, you can be sure you're not missing out anything.
2. Use Boomerang for Gmail to schedule replies and set up reminders to follow up on sent emails. Thus, you are in control of your time because you can send all your replies at once.
3. Don't write more than a paragraph of response to your email. A better and more effective option is to make a quick call, then, write a short email to act as the paper trail.

When I implemented this technique, I spend less than an hour on emails instead of two hours. I tracked my time using RescueTime,

5. Multitasking

Multitasking means switching between tasks constantly. As humans, our brains can't handle several complex tasks simultaneously. When you multitask, you are unproductive because you produce less quality work, make more mistakes and sometimes, lose more money.

How to overcome: Reread the previous sections in this chapter.

Chapter 5 - Dealing with Distractions

The Difference Between Internal and External Distractions

Before differentiating between internal and external distractions, here's an explanation about each of them.

Internal Distractions

Internal distractions are generated from our self-image and perceptions; they come from our inside. You are experiencing internal distractions each time your plan for a day is delayed or hindered by your thoughts or self-perceptions. Unruly negative ego (especially, lack of self-acceptance, lack of self-love, or both) is usually the primary cause of internal distractions. It involves your desire to be in control to change others or make specific changes about yourself. These thoughts eventually become a self-imposed internal struggle, which leads to frustration.

Compared to internal distractions, it is easier to overcome external distractions. You need to be in control of your mind to overcome internal distractions. That is, you must be mentally disciplined. When you have lots of things on your mind, you will be less productive. For example, you will struggle to focus when you have a health issue, are dehydrated or haven't gotten enough sleep. Also, if you are experiencing some challenges in your relationship, you will struggle to focus.

More importantly, internal distractions prevent you from doing actual work. When you don't have a real purpose or mission, you do nothing. If you don't spend sufficient time to consider your real goals (whether long-term or short-term goals), you won't do anything. You must spend the time to plan your week and days, then, commit to doing what moves you closer to your goals.

Thus, you will avoid sitting in a reactive mode, waiting for someone to provide you with what to come or for the world to work for you. Thus, you can manage your time properly and be truly productive. When you experience internal distractions (which is bound to happen), you must leave them for their proper time. Otherwise, you won't focus on being productive with your time.

External Distractions

There are a lot of external distractions that can affect your focus negatively. You need to pay attention to some of these distractions because they are vital.

Examples;

- Your child needs a ride home because she called in sick from school.
- Your best client needs your attention because he's struggling with a severe challenge

While these external distractions can and does happen, they are not frequent enough to affect your productivity. However, most external distractions shouldn't command your attention because they aren't that important. Examples of unimportant external distractions include countless novelties and trivialities on the internet or conversation about the walking dead, game of thrones or any other popular television shows.

Generally, everything else that you can use as an excuse not to plan or execute your plan is an external distraction.

If you are disciplined and thoughtful enough, you can shut down, turn off, and avoid external distractions.

You will discover proven ways to eliminate external distractions later in this chapter.

Types of Internal Distractions

In this section, you will discover the types of internal distractions that exist. The usual emphasis is on eliminating distractions, but you need to know the types of internal distractions before you can prevent or get rid of them. Knowing the types will help you to realize your kind of inner distraction and the best way to eliminate it.

Type 1: Self-doubt

Insecurity (and not lack of talent) is the biggest killer of dreams. You can turn your self-doubt to a self-fulfilling prophecy when you believe things such as:

"I can't compete with other businesses" or

"I'll never get promoted."

Regardless of your confidence, there are times you are going to experience a little self-doubt. It happens to all of us. However, you must be mentally healthy to prevent self-doubt so that you can achieve your goals.

Self-doubt makes you lose your self-confidence. Self-doubt can make you quit before reaching your goal. This is a significant distraction. Boosting your self-esteem is the best way to get rid of this inner distraction. A few ways you can improve your self-confidence are:

1. Staying focused on the present

For example, you are running out into an athletic field or on a stage, but within you, you're thinking, "I will embarrass myself." This thought will affect your performance negatively. Instead of allowing your inner monologue to pull you down, focus on the present. Remind yourself that you don't need to strive for perfection; you only need to do your best. Thus, you can pour in all your energy to achieve better performance.

2. Control your emotions

Your thoughts and actions are highly dependent on your emotions. Unless you take proactive measures to control your emotions, anxious feelings can trigger doubtful thoughts and mar your performance.

Monitor the influence of your emotions on your choices. Control your anxiety and calm your mind by distracting yourself with mundane tasks, going for a walk, or taking deep breaths. Don't cave in, give up, or bail out on account of your short-term discomfort.

3. Ask yourself, "What's the worst thing that can happen?"

Wild predictions such as "I'm going to mess up everything" can lead to self-doubt. When these doubtful thoughts start creeping in, consider the worst-case scenario. Should you make a mistake, how bad would be the consequences of your error? The truth is, any mistake is not likely to be life-altering. Failing to get a promotion, stumbling over your lines or losing a game won't be that relevant in a few years. So, calm your nerves by keeping things in proper perspective.

4. Consider the evidence supports your distracting thoughts

Ask yourself, "What's the proof that I can't or can do this?" Your answer to this question will give you a realistic perspective. Though this technique won't eliminate all your self-doubt, it will reduce it significantly.

5. Don't worry about a little self-doubt

According to a 2010 study published in the Psychology of Sport And Exercise, slight insecurity can lead to better performance. When you're aware that things might not go according to plan, create a few minutes to plan how you can improve. This few minutes of planning will help you, in the long run, to utilize your time correctly. Self-confidence remains the best way to eliminate self-distractions.

Type 2: Overthinking and distressful thoughts

If you're fretting about how you will succeed tomorrow or beating up yourself over a mistake you made yesterday. Then, you are suffering from distressful thoughts. Thus, you are in a constant state of anguish, and you are unable to get out of your head.

Though we all over-think things now and then, it shouldn't be too constant. Two of the destructive thought patterns in this internal monologue are worrying and ruminating.

Ruminating involves going over previous actions. Examples of ruminating thoughts include:

- I spoke up too soon at the meeting today. I could tell from their eyes that they thought I was an idiot.
- I was stupid to have left my old job. If I had stayed, I would have been happier.

- My parents were right. I won't amount to anything.

Worrying involves negative predictions about your future. Examples include:

- My presentation tomorrow will be embarrassing. Everyone will conclude that I'm not competent because my hands will be shaking and my face will turn red throughout the presentation.
- It doesn't matter what I do; my promotion will never happen.
- I'm no longer good enough for my spouse. He/she will divorce me and find someone else.
- I should help Edward with his task and destroy my time management plan for the day because Edward helped during my previous task.

Sometimes, distressful thoughts can be in the form of negative imaginations such as imagining your car veering off the road. Overthinking everything prevents you from taking any productive activity.

Effects of overthinking
Overthinking can have a severe negative impact on your well-being.

Evidence from an NCBI research suggests that you are more susceptible to mental health problems when you dwell on your problems, mistakes, or shortcomings. Your tendency to ruminate increases as your mental health declines, leading to a vicious cycle that you may never break.

Another study also showed that severe emotional distress could be the result of overthinking. When you can't sleep even after shutting your mind, then, you know you are an overthinker. With fewer hours of sleep and more reduced sleep quality, your time management for the next day will completely poor because you will desire more rest.

Type 3: Shiny object syndrome

Shiny object syndrome involves distraction through new products, tools, and ideas. These 'bright shiny objects' seem more fun and more exciting than your current projects. Sometimes, you may even think this new project has more prospects than the project you are working on at the moment.

If you can relate to any of the following, then, you are suffering from shiny object syndrome:

- Rather than complete what you are currently doing, you continuously jump from one goal to another
- You are fascinated by the wild claims of various e-courses. Thus, you jump to another e-course without implementing what you learn from the previous one.
- Instead of executing one of your business ideas, you keep compiling a list of business ideas.
- Rather than build the basics, you spend too much time on new ideas and tools, 95% of which is noise.

One of the best ways to overcome shiny object syndrome is getting into the habit of completing a task before moving to the next one. In the next section of this chapter, you will discover proven ways to silence internal distractions.

13 Ways to Silence Internal Distractions

In the previous section, we discussed the types of internal distractions, but we didn't discuss how to stop them except for the first type of distraction. In this section, you will discover how to silence types two and three internal distractions. Also, you will find other ways to silence internal distractions.

4 Ways to Stop Overthinking

You can limit your negative thinking patterns with consistent practice. Here are the six proven ways to stop overthinking:

1. Start paying attention to the way you think

The first step to putting an end to overthinking is awareness. When you observe that you're replaying events in your mind repeatedly, bring yourself to the conscious fact that your thoughts can't change the past.

2. Learn to recognize and replace thinking errors

Since negative thoughts can be highly exaggerated, you must acknowledge and replace them with positive thoughts. Otherwise, you may erroneously assume that you will be fired for calling in sick or that you will become homeless because you forget a deadline.

3. Focus on solving the problem

Looking for solutions is more helpful than dwelling on your problems. Deduce lessons from a mistake or develop steps to prevent a future issue. Always ask yourself, what can I do about it? Rather than asking, why did this happen?

4. Create time to reflect

A little time of reflection can help you to manage your time for the rest of the day properly. Through your meditation, you should identify possible holes in your plan or what you could differently to be successful. Your daily schedule should include 20 minutes of thinking time. Allow your mind to wander excessively during this time. Then, when the 20 minutes is up, move into productive tasks. When you observe that you've started overthinking outside your thinking time, remind yourself that you will think about it later. You may have to repeat this reminder more than once before it becomes effective.

5 Tips to Overcome Shiny Object Syndrome

It is when you are focused that you can manage your time satisfactorily and get things done. But you need to avoid shiny object syndrome before you can become entirely focused. Here are five proven tips to overcome shiny object syndrome:

1. Learn to differentiate between real opportunities and shiny objects

Shiny objects are actual distractions that disguise as excellent and exciting tools. For example, some new tools are being introduced into the market that makes a lot of bold claims. But won't add value to your productive work or life. Real opportunities must have an actual impact on your life or work. For example, tools that improve your product or service delivery and tools that can boost your workflow.

2. Use the "wait and see" technique

Use this technique when you're unsure about your next decision. Many tools are fast becoming obsolete within a couple of years due to rapid technological advancements. If new software is introduced into the market and claiming to make you more productive, critically analyze whether or not you need that tool. You should only buy this new tool when you are sure that you have no alternative.

3. Remove low-quality information sources

Managing sources of distraction is one of the best ways to manage distraction. When you subscribe to newsletters that recommend new products frequently, you will always struggle to focus because you want to assess each product before making a purchase decision. This is called cognitive load. Your best option is to remove low-quality information sources rather than using your precious mental energy to sieve out the noise. Evaluate your email subscriptions, Facebook group memberships, and social media news feeds. Unsubscribe from groups and newsletters that offer unhelpful, irrelevant suggestions.

4. Don't follow the bandwagon

Assess the suitability of a new tool for your work and life before buying it. Don't buy it or use it because your colleagues are calling it the best thing to happen since sliced bread. This new tool can become your source of unproductivity. Always ask yourself these three critical questions:

- What are the merits vs. demerits of doing this?
- What value will this add to my life or work?
- Do I need it?

If you are genuinely sure that it will add value to your work and life, then, do it.

5. Don't waste your time chasing trends

If you continuously follow every new tool and idea, you won't get things done. You will only be wasting your time chasing trends. Also, understand that a new product doesn't mean it's a better product.

4 Other Ways to Overcome Internal Distractions

Now, here are four other ways to silence any form of internal distractions:

1. Practice cognitive defusion

Most of our intrusive thoughts are rhetorical and abstract. One effective way to lose the power of your negative thoughts is to reframe those thoughts until they lose their meaning. Cognitive defusion is a technique that changes a word or phrase and how it impacts you. For example, if you always repeat a phrase such as "life is meaningless," you can reframe it to "I'm having a thought that life is meaningless." Repeating the reframed sentence removes any negativity out of it. Similarly, if you hear a word in your head repeatedly when you feel inadequate ('loser') or mess up ('stupid'), saying it out repeatedly dilutes its power. The key is to verbalize the thought so that you can hear it.

A similar technique to cognitive defusion is called the positive effect or positive direction. As the name suggests, this technique involves reframing negative words into positive words. You can turn words such as "I can't do this" into "Of course, I can be successful." "I will never achieve this goal" becomes "I'm definitely going to make this happen." When you use such positive phrasing, you prime your frontal lobes and consequently, stimulate a goal-directed behavior.

2. *Practice self-compassion*
Self-compassion is the act of treating yourself with kindness. You use a gentle understanding and soothing to respond to your anxiety. When you start having anxious thoughts such as "Oh no, here we go. I can't take this. I hate these thoughts."

Self-compassion can turn this internal dialogue to "It's not easy to feel this way, but you can overcome these problems and complete the task." This technique lessens the effects of the anxiety by encouraging you not to blame yourself for feeling anxious. It helps you to approach the fear from a place of understanding.

3. *Verbalize your thoughts*
Since what's floating in your head is often a bunch of unordered thoughts and worries, talking in your head rarely reveals

anything significant. However, when you verbalize your feelings and fears, you can develop a story and identify the meaning of the story. If you don't like to a person, journal it. The effects are similar.

Writing helps with physical and psychological issues since it leads to the development of a coherent narrative over time. It is the cognitive processing during writing that makes it a therapeutic activity. By creating a description, you can have an idea of what's happening. Hence, reducing part of those awful cycle of mind chatter.

Another writing technique is to write out the tasks you want to achieve within the next hour. Then, set a deadline for you to finish the tasks. The act of writing out your critical hourly tasks will refocus your brain on your most vital projects. Adding a deadline creates a sense of urgency that helps you to remain focused.

4. *Practice mindfulness and meditation*
If you're stuck in your head and need a quick grounding in the present, mindfulness can be more accessible. It is slightly different from meditation. The best description of mindfulness is by Jon Kabat-Zinn, *"Focus on the present moment on purpose without being judgmental."*

At every moment, always refocus your attention on what you're doing at that moment. Take a moment to focus on the present instead of what's in your head. Thus, you can snap yourself out of your internal distractions when it happens.

6 Reliable Ways to Defeat External Distractions

External distractions usually derails our daily work ethic. This can be anything from your neighbor's little child running past your office window, an unexpected knock on the front door, or a colleague stopping by for a chat. You could be distracted by notifications from Skype, social media newsfeeds, or email.

Most times, we are at fault for these distractions. Most of us are guilty of checking Facebook newsfeeds or email when we should be doing actual work. At other times, distractions happen just like life happens. Hence, you must regain your concentration instantly to prevent the busyness from consuming your minds.

Since prevention is better than cure, you must find proven ways to minimize these distractions. When our attempts to prevent distractions fail, it's crucial that you have strategies in place to deal with them. Here are six reliable ways of defeating external distractions:

1. Attention firewalling

In recent years, famous figures such as Merlin Mann, Gina Trapani, and Tim Ferriss have made this concept popular in productivity circles. This technique involves preventing distractions rather than dealing with it.

You must track your activities and identify the distractions that prevent you from doing productive work. For instance, you can use software to block access to a specific website that wastes too much of your time. If it remains a distraction because you could bypass the software. You can prevent it by using your router. Since you will need to reset the router and save the change, it would be a bit harder to bypass the router. During that time, you won't be distracted by the internet, and you have a high probability of focusing and refocusing on your tasks when you are distracted.

For email, uninstall notifiers and change the settings of your phone to silent to avoid the beeping sounds of new messages.

2. Keep your to-do list readily visible

Keeping your to-do list nearby makes it easier to get back on task during your waiting period and keep your focus clear. Hence, you can avoid falling into the distraction trap. Also, ensure you write your to-do list legible such that you can read it from your most common working position.

Set up little reminder messages such as "are you on task?" to help you regain focus during times you start wandering. The real secret is to make your task list visible all the time and be mindful of it.

3. Keep a procrastination pad.

This procrastination pad can be by your desk or on your computer. Jot notes about your distractions in them as they come. Thus, you can forget about them and come back to them later. An alternative is to use a separate device to store your distractions. For example, you can have a jotter titled "procrastination pad," which contains your distractions.

4. Maximize your productivity peaks

We all have specific periods of the day where we are at peak productivity. You need to identify these times and give yourself the best advantage by scheduling your most important for these times.

5. Psyche yourself up to work

A compelling reason to complete work is highly essential in staying on task. Remind yourself about the benefits of finishing your task. For example, a work-free weekend or the pride in finishing a challenging project. Reminding yourself of some short-term benefits also works. For example, if you complete a specific amount of work, you can have enough time to rest and take your wife on a date for the night.

6. *Use the instant-reward technique*

Tell yourself you would do something entertaining for 10 minutes once you can complete your next task within a specific timeframe. For example, if you complete 600 words of an article within the next 30 minutes, you will play your favorite game on your phone for 5 minutes. If your work allows you to work remotely, you can use this technique to sharpen your focus. However, this method should be your last resort because it's almost impossible to do your best work within 20- or 30-minute timeframes. It's a good strategy when you are too distracted or when you struggle to start your day with productive work.

Chapter 6 - Emulating Success

Goal Setting Examples from The Business Masters

In this section, we explore the goal-setting secrets of some great business executives. Let's get started:

1. Barbara Corcoran

Barbara is a "Shark Tank" investor and founder of Barbara Corcoran Inc.

"Due to time constraints, I usually organize my list in sections. The first section is for calls I intend to make, but it doesn't exceed three calls. I put my calls into the first section to avoid forgetting about them.

The review section is my second section. These are typically short tasks. In it, I answer questions such as 'Would you like to be on our show?' I can do a quick review and get it out of the way since the relevant paperwork is attached to it. Though they are not listed in any particular order, I ensure I complete them in less than a day.

The third section is my project list. These contain tasks that move my business forward and make me money. I further categorize them as A, B, and C, depending on importance. Some of the tasks in this list are companies I've invested in through Shark Tank. *The A tasks are essential and today-only. The B tasks are also necessary, but their deadline is not today.*

When my task list is too small, it shows that I haven't created time for reflection. My list grows more substantial when I have more time to reflect. When I reflect, I'm able to think of new opportunities that I don't want to forget. Despite trying various to-do lists, my useful to-do lists have been the ones typed or written.

There is a satisfaction that I get with crossing off tasks that I can't get with using the delete button."

2. Jim McCann

Jim is the author of *Talk is (Not) Cheap: The Art of Conversation Leadership* and the founder and CEO of 1-800-flowers.com, Inc.

"I've been using lists for most parts of my business life. I had a crazy list-maker as a mentor at St. John's home in Queens, New York. Being busy is easy, but being effective is a lot harder. Using my mentor's example, I bought a pad and printed 'things I have to do today' on it. Currently, I combine physical and digital pads. My list is divided into four:

- Things I must do today
- A general to-do list
- A projects list
- A long-term ideas list. These are highly important for the company's growth.

Before assigning my jottings to any of the lists above, I ask myself one question: 'Must it be done today?' Most of these jottings are useful ideas that fit for the long-term ideas list or the projects list. My team assesses these lists from time to time to determine whether or not the ideas are still good enough for implementation. We replace the ideas that are no longer good enough with new ones. With a proper task list, you can become a better manager of your time."

3. Jim Koch

Jim Koch is the founder of the Boston Beer Company.

"Priority tasks from different internal teams determine my day. Every morning, I write down a maximum of five must-do goals for that day on a Post-it note. This act keeps me focused for the day.

While these items not necessarily urgent, they are important. Once I start my day, I ensure that the list remains reachable to avoid procrastinating on them. However, I strike out all items on the list by the close of each day. Also, each of my weeks starts with a maximum of five emails in my inbox. To ensure that issues or questions are resolved pretty quickly, I respond to emails almost immediately after I receive them. Thus, responding to emails doesn't affect my productivity during my daily breaks.

During my break-time, I switch off my internet and spend that time at the nearest hardware store. I may even pick up a tool I need at home. By the time I return to my desk, I will make headway with my previous issue or dilemma."

4. Daymond John

Daymond is the founder of the famous clothing line, FUBU, and he is the author of the *Power of Broke*.

"I have a set of 10 goals. The first seven goals are 6-month goals. The rest are 5-year, 10-year, and 20-year goals. Since I want my goals to be the last thing I think and dream about, I make it a habit to read my goals every morning and every night. I write down the seven goals on a piece of paper. While each goal has an expiry date, I include a few details of how I will achieve each goal. The first five goals are health, family, business, relationship, and philanthropy goals. The next two are personal financial goals and business project goals. Each goal is written in a positive language. For example, if my goal is to reduce my weight to 170 pounds by July 5. The few details would be to eat fish, drink eight glasses of water daily, and exercise twice per day. It won't include avoiding alcohol, meat, and fried foods."

5. Yunha Kim

Yunha is the founder and CEO of Simple Habit, a meditation app.

"Setting time limits is one of my workflow secrets. We often have never-ending lists of to-dos at a startup like ours. Hence, it is not feasible to fully finish a task in one sitting."

13 Time Management Hacks of Successful People

It is not easy to manage or maximize your time. But by knowing the tips and tricks of today's most successful people, you can use their tips or develop your time management strategies. Thus, improving your productivity. Learn more about various unconventional time-saving tricks from the time management tricks of some of the world's most successful people.

1. Sir Richard Branson delegates emails

Sir Richard is the founder of the Virgin group. He is also a British business magnate, investor, author, and philanthropist.

"I check reader emails in the morning. I pass some to colleagues, dictate the ones with quick answers to my assistants. But I write the more detailed responses personally. I check my email in bursts to focus on my current tasks. I give my employees space rather than directives. I am comfortable allowing them to take responsibility because I hired people I trust."

2. Jack Dorsey creates daily themes

Jack is the CEO and co-founder of payment processing experts, Square and social media company, Twitter. Dorsey runs these two significant companies simultaneously by giving each day a theme. Dorsey spends each day of the week to focus on a particular primary area. For example, Mondays can be for product development, and Tuesdays can be for general management functions. Wednesdays can be buffer days where you respond to low-priority emails and tasks.

3. Mary Callahan Erdoes uses the calendar for day-to-day management

"The biggest tool to manage time is calendar management. Focus on controlling your calendar. Create a list of you expect from others and what others expect from you. If you don't control your calendar, it will end up controlling you."

4. Barack Obama limits his outfits

Barack Obama is the former president of the united states.

"I pare down decisions by wearing only blue or gray suits. Since I have too many decisions to make, I prefer to exclude eating and wearing decisions out of it by paring down my decisions."

5. Jack Groetzinger tracks his time

Jack is the co-founder and CEO of SeatGeek.

"I have an estimated period for each of my tasks. I have software that records when I start and finish each item on my task list. I push myself to accomplish an efficiency goal for each day. My efficiency goal is actual minutes divided by expected minutes. I have fun gamifying my to-do list because I own all the spots on the leaderboard."

6. Gary Vaynerchuk uses other people's time

Gary Vaynerchuk is a business coach and the CEO of VaynerchukMedia.

"I scale my time efficiency using other people. I can focus on my personal and professional priorities by having others do the tasks that must be done. One of my assistants works full-time as my health coach. He oversees my exercise and nutrition. The other assistant follows me around and films me. As my time becomes more valuable, I may hire a full-time driver rather than waiting for a ride."

Pro Tip: If you can't afford to hire full-time assistants, you can hire virtual assistants or outsource some of your tasks to them.

7. Steve Ballmer creates a time budget

Steve is the ex-CEO of Microsoft. Steve has a spreadsheet accessible by his assistants where he budgets time to those who need to speak with him or meet him. Thus, he manages his time by spending most of his time on important things.

8. Adora Cheung is strict about meetings

Adora Cheung is the CEO of Homejoy, an online platform that connects customers with home service providers. Adora sends a Google Doc to potential meeting participants. These participants write down the agenda for the meeting. After prioritizing the topics, Adora does not discuss any plan that's not on the list.

9. Tony Hsieh uses Yesterbox

Tony Hsieh is the CEO of the famous shoe and clothing line, Zappos. Tony recommends responding to yesterday's emails today. Hence, today's emails won't clutter your focus for the day. He terms this technique as "Yesterbox." One capable app that can help you to achieve inbox zero is called boomerang. It helps you to give proper attention to specific emails by resending those emails into your inbox as new emails at your specified time.

10. Arianna Huffington eats meals away from her desk

Arianna Huffington is the author of 15 books, the founder of the *Huffington Post* and the founder/CEO of Thrive Global. She recommends *not* working while taking meal breaks during the day. "*Take a colleague and have lunch at a table far away from your desk or go to a cafeteria. This shouldn't take more than 20 minutes. Doing this is more recharging than eating lunch while working, which is what many of us do. It can be the difference between having a productive or an unproductive end to your day."*

11. Mark Cuban uses email for most interactions

Mark Cuban is an American investor and businessman. He co-owns 2929 Entertainment, owns the Dallas Mavericks (an American basketball team), and is an investor in "Shark Tank." Rather than waste time in long meetings or on lengthy phone calls, Mark Cuban uses email for most conversations and become more productive. *"Email saves me hours every day. No phone calls, no meetings, and I set my schedule. Unless I'm picking up a check, all other things are email. I love it, and I live on it."*

12. Jeff Bezos uses the "Two Pizza Rule"

Jeff is the founder, CEO, and president of Amazon.com. He is also an investor and charity donor. Rather than waste his time in meetings, Bezos maximizes his time by not attending big meetings. To him, a meeting is big if two pizzas can't feed the participants at the meetings.

13. Nick Huzar capitalizes on Sundays

Nick is the CEO and co-founder of OfferUp, which connects local buyers and sellers. *"Plan your work and stick to the plan. I ensure that I create a quiet period for myself on Sundays. During this period, I examine each department at OfferUp to determine the team's priorities. Then, during the week, I support each team to implement these priorities. Also, I'm a sucker for routines. With routines, I'm able to eliminate excuses. For example, the first thing I always do each night is to pack for the next day's gym."*

10 Morning Routines of Groundbreaking Entrepreneurs

Starting your day right is the key to uber-productive days. Your actions at the start of the day will determine whether you will achieve extraordinary or mediocre results. Here's how ten highly successful entrepreneurs maximize their days right from the time they get out of bed.

1. Create a to-do list the previous night

"On alternating days, I work out for an hour and jog to the office. While at the office, I review my to-do list from the previous night. Thus, I can identify my most important tasks and finish them before anything else." - Barbara Corcoran, founder of the Corcoran Group.

2. Start your day with maximum energy

"By waking up early and playing basketball, my starts with the right energy and clarity. After showering, I eat a 3-egg breakfast, which fills me to satisfaction and sharpens my focus. Then, I proceed to achieve a zero-inbox. I help my team with any challenges they're facing. Thus, I have an idea of my challenges for the day. I ponder on my tasks' list for the day and face them squarely." - Tim Draper, founding partner of DFJ - a legendary VC firm.

3. Choose a routine that fits your personality type

"Your personality type can be emotional, social, action, or practical. If you are the emotional type, you are sensitive and might be introverted. Hence, your routine will involve lots of quiet time and introspection. If you are the social type, your daily routine will be people-based. For example, you will love working out in the gym in the presence of at least five people. If you are the action-type

personality, you will love a morning routine of variety. You will love to start your day with a combination of jogging, jujitsu, or reading various books, especially books outside your industry. Practical-type people love a well-structured daily routine. The most important aspect of any routine is sticking with your plan. We all tend to have a morning routine until life happens. So, use your personality type to determine your most effective morning routine." - Tai Lopez, investor and advisor to many multimillion-dollar businesses with an eight-figure online empire.

4. Tune up your brain

"Since I know my day will be busy and probably, unpredictable, I start my day by going for a cold swim in the pool. Then, over a cup of coffee, I play the crossword puzzle in the Los Angeles Times; this rarely exceeds 20 minutes. Then, I get into my office to start working." - Mark Sisson. Mark Sisson is the publisher of marksdailyapple.com (a paleo blog), the best-selling author of the New Primal Blueprint and the founder of the Primal Blueprint.

5. Use nutrition to fire up your brain

"I drink one ounce of water which contains a cleansing mineral. I flush out my system by drinking a quart of structured purified water. Then, I wake up every muscle with a 45-pound kettlebell and 20 minutes of Turkish getups. I provide my brain with the ultimate brain nutrient by taking three milliliters of oceans alive marine phytoplankton. After my shower, I use 30 sprays of ease magnesium for my abdomen before taking a supplement to repair my cells. I eat two farm-fertilized organic chicken eggs and three different types of fruit for my breakfast. Lastly, I take a cup of green smoothie." - Ian Clark. Ian is the founder and CEO of Activation Products.

6. Jumpstart your metabolism

"After getting out of bed by 5:30 am, I drink 20 ounces of water to set my metabolism into action. I write my gratitude list for the morning. Then, I determine my two main priorities for the day. These priorities must move me in the direction of my goals before I can call my day awesome." - Jon Braddock, founder, and CEO of My Life & Wishes.

7. Verbalize your day's intention

"I spend a few minutes to show gratitude for health and body before I get out of bed. Then, I speak out my intention for the day. While setting the intentions for my goals, I drink a glass of water, light some candles, and daydream. I check my emails for important messages before swinging into full work mode." - Elle Russ, Coach and Best-Selling Author of the Paleo Thyroid Solution.

8. Start early

"I get up at 4:15 am and spend 15 minutes of gratitude. By 5 am, I am at the gym to have a bodybuilding session with a personal trainer until 6 am. Between 6:30 and 7 am, I meditate and envision how to achieve my goals and dreams. I spend 30 minutes (7:15 am to 7:45 am) with my family before starting work by 8 am." - Adele McLay, Author, Speaker, and Business Growth Consultant.

9. Start with meditation

"After meditation, I use my five-minute journal before exercising and drinking a protein shake. Then, I help others in my way. Either by making an important introduction, sending a written note of gratitude or posting a #ploughshare online. I spend some time to write or draw images. Lastly, I take one major step to achieve my goal." - Chris Plough, Serial Entrepreneur and Entrepreneur Advisor.

10. Block off times of solitude

"Being a father of young children, an entrepreneur, and a doctor, my days can become highly disorder without proper planning. After getting up by 6:30 am, I spend a minimum of 30 minutes in complete and peaceful solitude before having a cup of coffee. To get into the right state of mind, I pray, read some educational materials, review my goals for that day, and practice mindful meditation. I strongly engage in a positive-thinking mental state to foster immense power into my mind. When I am not on intermittent fasting, my breakfast is usually light and consists of a few nutritional supplements depending on my current blood test results. Then, I maximize the day by working with full zeal and energy." - Dr. Nick Zurowski, founder of NuVision Health Center.

I encourage you to use any of these morning routines as they are or more importantly, modify them to suit your lifestyle so that you can enjoy more productive and creative mornings.

Chapter 7 - Regaining Control of The Future

15 Effective Time Management Habits

If you have read this far, you would have identified some time management habits already. Some were discussed in the previous chapter as examples from business masters, successful people, and groundbreaking entrepreneurs. Others have been discussed in previous chapters. Hence, they won't be repeated in this chapter. Instead, you will discover more proven time management tips that you can incorporate into your daily life.

1. Learn to speed-read

While you cannot avoid all the barrage of information being thrown at you, you can sort them and go through them at your pace and time. Learning to speed-read is one of the most important skills you can develop. Have you ever taken a course in speed reading? If no, enroll for one now. With new technologies now available, you can read up to 1,000 words per minute and comprehend most of what you have read.

2. Stack your reading

Print and file important pieces of information, summaries, or valuable items. Alternatively, you can collate them in a separate file on your computer and read them later. Rather than lose focus on your current task, you can file away that piece of information and read them later. Once this becomes a habit, you will be amazed at how much you can give to what you read and how much more you read. Whether you are reading the paper version or electronic version of your newspapers, skim and read what's relevant to you. When you are reading the news, bear in mind that most of the information is always in the headline and first paragraph. Most times, you rarely need to read the remaining details to understand the story fully.

3. Only read what is important and relevant

The design of all magazines and newspapers is to make you read each page of the magazine or newspaper. The reason is for you to view all the advertisements in magazines or newspapers. Thus, you must read what matters to you only. After reviewing the table of contents, head to the information that is relevant to your life and work. The "rip and read" technique is an exceptional technique for printed materials. Rip out and file articles you intend to read. Then, carry the file with you to read during your timeouts. Similarly, read book reviews before spending time to read the complete book. You can get the main gist of the book by reading the book's review. Instead of scouring the web to read reviews, it is more convenient to subscribe to book review services.

4. Organize your work environment

For many people, they believe that a messy work environment and a cluttered desk aids their work efficiency. However, various research has shown that when people work in a clean, ordered environment and focus only on one task, their productivity almost triples instantly. People with a cluttered work environment spend copious time seeking the materials they need to work effectively. Psychologically, a cluttered work environment affirms your belief that you lack organization. Hence, you are continuously distracted by all the items you are seeing.

5. Maximize your mornings

Set your alarm clock for a couple of hours earlier than normal when you have deadlines to hit and projects to complete. I've found this to be more effective than trying to work extra in the evening when you're too tired to focus. You can get some dedicated time by going to bed an hour earlier than your usual time. In the early morning hours, your mind is alert, you're refreshed, the house is quiet, and you are at peak productivity. Spend this extra hour on one item of your task list. A half-hour earlier in the day is an additional 23 days over the year. This is as good as buying time. Imagine that!

6. Map out your weekly meals

Consider your schedules, special occasions, and items on the grocery list to plan your meal for the week. Remember to review the pantry to ensure that all the ingredients for items on your grocery list are completely available. Also, go to the supermarket with a proper plan, there should be no impulse purchase. When you make it a habit to plan your meal once a week, you won't waste time pondering on what to eat. A side benefit is that you eat healthier.

You can apply the weekly meal plan to other aspects of your life. For example, choose a day to plan the clothes you will wear for the week. Then, ensure you wash them and make them ready for your use.

7. Be in the present

Abandon all your baggage from the previous day in the past. Don't allow your previous day's failures, embarrassments, losses, disappointments, and mistakes to affect the joy you will likely experience today. Start your day by expecting to experience a day of relationship building, fulfillment, and success. Maximize your time to enjoy the best return on each day of your life.

8. Establish rules for your time

Establish rules for your time when creating your schedule. Turn off your cell phone during your timeout, for example, during breakfast. Set aside blocks of time that you will not be available to people and devices.

9. Audit your time

Assess your current time spending habits for the next seven days. Record your activities in a journal or on your phone. Split your activities into one-hour blocks. Then, answer the following questions:

- What did you accomplish?
- Was it a complete waste of time?
- Did you spend the time to your satisfaction?

Use the priority matrix discussed in chapter four to log your activities in the appropriate quadrant. Add the numbers after seven days. So, which quadrant did you spend the most time? Don't be surprised by your answer.

10. Eliminate your bad habits

Bad habits are one of our biggest time wasters. Those bad habits eliminate our precious little time. Hence, if you are serious about achieving big goals in your life, and spend your time wisely, ensure you eliminate those bad habits. Examples of time-wasting habits include going out to drink with friends frequently, playing games, excessively surfing social media, and Netflix binge-watching.

11. Find a mentor

When you don't have someone to guide you, you can quickly get distracted and dissuaded. But it's easier to stay on track with your time when you can personally rely on someone who's been through the same process. Thus, he can help you achieve your goals faster.

12. Don't wait for inspiration

You are wasting time by waiting to start a project. Since there is no perfect time to do anything, throw away the excuses that are preventing you from getting started. While I'm not suggesting that you should be impatient, you should identify what you intend to accomplish and take immediate action towards it.

13. Engage in hobbies

Hobbies engage in parts of your brain that you don't use for work. Thus, you become more creative and can solve problems with ease. You can achieve success by spending some time outside of your comfort zone. If you're a software developer, go out and socialize. If you're pianist, practice martial arts. If you're a lawyer, learn to dance.

14. Have a great time

Don't become obsessed about marking off all the tasks on your task list. Balance your work and life to enjoy your day. It's not worth it to complete an oversized workload one day only to have an unproductive, burnt-out day the next day. Work at your best pace. When you rush through tasks, you become stressed and produce substandard work.

15. Meditate

A few minutes of meditation can improve your focus and calmness. Thus, your work becomes more efficient, and your contribution is more significant. Also, meditation brings your mind back to the present to help you avoid several distractions. When your mind is in the present, you can accomplish a lot more within a small time-span. Meditation improves your awareness. Thus, we rarely make mistakes at work, and you save the time you're supposed to use to correct your errors. Meditation can also strengthen your intuition. A strong intuition enhances your decision-making ability and consequently, saves you time.

Defeating Perfectionism Once and for All

Though our current world expects us to be perfect in always, it doesn't mean that perfectionism is the way to a successful life. Like an obsessive-compulsive disorder, your desire for perfection can mess you up. And since it makes you lose perspective as you get deeper into it, it messes up those around you. Since none of us can become perfect, you will only be driving yourself crazy, trying to achieve an elusive goal. Perfectionism can lead to depression. Research by Sydney Blatt, a psychologist at Yale University showed that perfectionists are more likely to kill themselves than regular people.

To avoid the perfectionist trap, implement these seven proven steps:

1. Practice failing

Doing exercises where you will likely fail is one of the most effective ways to defeat perfectionism. So, learn a new skill that requires a lot of falling and embarrassment. It will teach you that tolerance of failure, self-compassion, and patience are part of the learning curve.

For example, I joined a racing group of paddlers despite having been on a paddleboard only a couple of times. This group consists of people who paddle at least 21 miles in the ocean and perform those cool 360 turns on their boards. I spent most of the evening in the water and not on it, but I am now more comfortable with failing. I realize that the world won't end because I am the worst person in a group of athletes. I will do my best to translate this lesson into other areas of my life, where I am anxious or depressed due to perfectionism.

2. Differentiate between goals and dreams

Since it is highly probable that they won't happen, grand ideas usually create lots of angst. For example, one of my friends used to dream of playing professional basketball. Nothing wrong in having a dream, right? But he started having behavioral issues because he was placed in the C team of his basketball team. When he's on his good behavior, he will practice his shots and improve his techniques for hours daily. But he always plays badly during games because he was exerting too much pressure on himself. When I feel like my expectations were weighing too much on me, I usually write down my goals on a piece of paper. Then, I will check off the realistic ones. But I will tweak the silly ones to avoid putting myself under undue pressure.

3. Be a hard worker

It is often said that smart people cut corners. However, knowing which corners to cut is the art of being a star performer. Hence, the way out is to analyze your goal in all honesty critically. Then, identify any perfectionism in the plan for each purpose. Most times, we hide under perfectionism to avoid taking actions to accomplish our real goals. The truth is, a proper plan, hard work, and a bit of luck are required to achieve any real intent. But most perfectionists don't agree that luck is involved in achieving any goal.

4. Keep yourself in check

Keep yourself in check when your self-doubt is becoming more real, or you start having reasons to believe your inner critic. Use these questions to give yourself a reality check:

- Are my thoughts based on facts, or are they the figment of my imagination?
- Why am I making unfavorable verdicts?
- Is the situation as bad as I imagine it?

- What's the worst thing that can happen? Is it likely to happen?
- Will this be important in the next five years? Will this be an issue at vital moments of my life? Examples of essential moments include childbirth, moving to another city, or moving abroad.

By the time I complete answering these questions, I often realize that I was only trying to validate various falsehoods in my head. Sometimes, I even forgot how I got into this frightening state in the first place. Apart from giving reassuring our self-esteem, this reality test also makes less dependent on others for affirmative compliments.

5. Be kind to yourself

As a perfectionist, you often criticize others. It is a proven fact that this criticism is a defense mechanism. It causes you to pick on the shortcomings in others rather than accept those shortcomings in yourself or accept that no human being is perfect. The more you identify your weaknesses, the more you look out for it in those around you. You do this because you have created an ideal image of the perfect person and life, but you can't seem to separate this idealized version from reality. A simple and effective way to reduce this habit significantly is to be kind to yourself. When you like your "flawed and imperfect" self, you're much less likely to be the irritable person who critically analyzes others.

So, try saying one thing you love about yourself each morning. It can be something about your face or a poem about yourself. Anytime you feel you need a boost during the day, repeat this affirmation. Note that nothing stops you from using the same declaration every day or having seven daily affirmations. Thus, you only repeat one affirmation every seven days. Rather than living an unforgiving, locked-down, and hard-hearted life, start being kind to yourself.

6. Refuse fear

Are you afraid of:

- Choosing a partner,
- Making the wrong life decision or
- Starting a new project?

If yes, then, you are exhibiting some of a perfectionist's trait. All the factors above have a common theme: a fear of failure. Thus, we rely on others to guide us and make our decisions for us. But refusing to allow fear to dictate your moves or choice is one of the best ways to combat such behavior.

One way to develop the habit of preventing fear to lead is to automate the start of the sequence. For example, a basketball player is ready to rise and shoot just as he has done a hundred times a day during practice by coming to the free-throw line, touching his socks, shorts, receiving the ball and bouncing it exactly three times.

Similarly, a pro golfer may be chatting with the scorekeeper, a friendly official, his playing partner or his caddie while walking along the fairway. But the moment he stands behind the ball and takes a deep breath, he's telling himself just one thing: focus.

In each of these examples, the athletes were able to replace doubt and fear with comfort and routine. They could do this because they've learned how to automate the start of their sequence. Rather than pretend not to be in the mood because I am afraid to start, I start with the smallest step towards the goal.

7. Be proud of your accomplishments

When we were young, we sketched what we intend to become in the future. However,, most of us never become what we've sketched out. Rather than being an astronaut or petrochemical engineer, you are probably a barista who barely spends time with his loved ones because you work for long periods. As a perfectionist, you need to accept that fact. Stop comparing yourself with others thinking you haven't achieved enough or you may never achieve anything. Instead, be comfortable in your skin and be proud of your accomplishments.

Create a list of your accomplishments in the past week, month, or year. Even the simple things count. The book you finished, that small project you completed with your team or maintaining a clean home. These are your accomplishments without being the neuro-surgeon you imagined when you were five years old.

Like any change, trust and self-examination are some of the requirements to tame any perfectionist tendencies. But if you meet challenges on the way and it seems you aren't moving forward, don't beat yourself up or take yourself too seriously. Find the means to succeed and enjoy the process. Keep in mind that you are solely responsible for your success or failure. So, don't give up.

Tools and Techniques to Take Back Time for Good

Ever heard any or all of these phrases before:

- The emails flooding my inbox is making me lose focus.
- Let me check my social media feed. It won't take 5 minutes!

If you have heard any of these phrases, then, you know the person lacks proper time management. Time management involves organizing tasks and allocating time to specific activities (professional or personal).

Before delving into those tools and techniques, remember that tasks, time, people, and information are the four key areas to any successful time management system. Hence, you should have any of these four essential tools:

- **Notebook**

A good notebook is the most frequently missing too in people's time management systems. Yes, it is good to have a bunch of post-its or a pad of paper on your desk. But you should keep all your notes in one place. Thus, when you need to retrieve any piece of information, you can go to this place.

- **Address Book**

Most people do not see the value of a good address book because we now live in a uber-connected world. However, when you need to connect with valuable contact, LinkedIn, Instagram, Facebook, or Twitter may disappoint you. Your best option is to save all contact's phone numbers and email addresses in a safe place and treat them like gold.

- **Calendar**

If you don't know how and where you spend your time, it would be difficult to manage it. It is easier for you to schedule, plan, and track your time with a good calendar. You cannot only track the time for your meetings, but you can also track the time for your tasks and projects.

- **To-do list**

A good to-do list is a cornerstone of any productivity system. This one-time management tool should complete your arsenal of tools. However, don't forget to reread the common reasons why to-do lists fail in Chapter 3 of this book.

Thus, you can avoid making those mistakes with your to-do list. Lastly, your to-do list should be with you all the time. Double-check your time management toolkit to ensure that you have all these four essential time management tools.

When you can plan and accomplish your daily routines within specified time frames, then, you are a good manager of time. Thus, you can carry out your activities with more significant commitment. Fortunately, technology has made it possible to optimize every minute of the day. In this section, you will discover seven tools and techniques that I use, and I am convinced will improve your time management skills and productivity.

1. A time management system

A proper organization of your daily tasks is one of the steps you can take to improve your productivity and not suck at time management. In any self-organization process, creating to-do lists is an essential step. You might have to try a few to-do list methods to discover the one that's most suitable for you. Your to-do list could be a fancy electronic version on your mobile device or computer. But it could be done using old-fashioned pen and paper which you check off after completing each task.

An overview of each significant activity is your first step when you have high-level projects. Then, you can split them into specific tasks and arrange them in the order in which they have to be performed. Don't forget to add deadlines to each task.

Here are three examples of such systems that you can use

- **The Now Habit by Neil Fiore.** This system teaches you to use a reverse order to build your to-do list. Fill your calendar with realistic leisure time, committed activities, and scheduled chores. Then, use different lifestyle and scheduling rules to assign your tasks into the remaining times.
- **The Final Version by Mark Forster.** From the task list, you have written for the day, go through it, and identify the most crucial task. Complete that task, then, identify the next most important task. Complete it and repeat the process till you complete all the task for that day.
- **Getting Things Done by David Allen.** Perform a brain dump of your tasks on paper. Then, rearrange them in order of importance. Next, set a deadline for completion and get to work. Review your execution plans periodically and where necessary, make adjustments.

2. Wunderlist

With Wunderlist, you can create task lists, organize them into folders, and set up reminders to alert you when the deadline is close. Wunderlist has an enchanting user interface, and all its features work effectively on all devices (cell phone, tablet, or computer).

3. Remember The Milk

The free plan allows you to create tasks and synchronize them on any platform, including your emails. Thus, you can access your tasks anytime. Perfect for managing personal tasks, Remember The Milk is available for Android and iOS.

4. RescueTime

Do you always feel that time passes very quickly, and it's almost impossible for you to complete your daily activities? Then, the RescueTime app is your best option. With it, you can track your tasks online. It gauges your progress and reveals the time you spend procrastinating.

5. Todoist or Trello

Todoist is both a cloud-based app and a mobile app. You can access your Todoist tasks on multiple operating systems and even share your tasks with other colleagues. Also, it displays delivery times. You can easily play around with the features because it has an intuitive layout. First, type in your project, then, split them into specific tasks and attach a deadline to each of them. Now, assign a level of priority to each task (there are four priority levels there). You can move the tasks around to suit your available time.

If you have a small team, you can use Trello to visualize your team's projects. Within Trello, you can assign tasks to each team member, set up boards that represent projects and set up various lists within each board. There are a series of cards for each list. The cards represent tasks. For example, you can create a board for a specific project, split the board into lists (the stages of the project), then, arrange each individual's tasks on a series of cards.

6. Relaxation breaks

You must take time out of your work; it will increase your productivity. After a period of sustained concentration, your body needs a release, and your mind needs a timeout. Sometimes, you develop fresh ideas from your timeout. The best way to help this process is to take a 5-minute walk away from your workspace. If you don't take breaks intentionally, your mind will do so for you by wandering when you are tired.

Use the FocusMe app to set enforced breaks or break reminders.

7. Process management technique

When you have personal tasks or business tasks, then, the time management tools and techniques discussed above are excellent. However, when your business grows, and you need to manage bulk processes or team time, then, the process management technique is a more effective system. This technique maps out the primary operations of a company and set deadlines for each task. Also, it adds an alert configuration to serve as the basis of prioritization. Here's how the alert configuration works for an airfare booking task:

- The person in charge receives an email when you reach 50% of the task deadline
- You will see a red visual indicator when you reach 70% of the task deadline
- At 80% of the task deadline, the person in charge receives a new message.

8. Evernote

This free productivity tool allows you to organize your images, thoughts, and ideas in various formats (audio, text, or pictures). Also, you can record your speeches, interviews, and meetings. You can even share your voice or text attachments with your friends. Optimize your time by syncing the Remember The Milk app with Evernote. Arguably, one of Evernote's most useful and popular features is its web clipper. This is similar to bookmarks in web browsers. Web clipper allows you to "clip" paragraphs of text, images or entire webpages to Evernote. Clipped items can be organized, stored, and searched like regular notes. You can even add annotations to "clipped" items in Evernote. You can integrate Evernote with Gmail, Outlook, Google Drive, Microsoft teams, Salesforce, Slack, and most other apps on your mobile devices or PC.

9. MyLifeOrganized (MLO)

If you struggle to organize your goals, work with your to-do lists, or manage all your tasks, this app is your best option. This productivity tool helps you to focus on the actual steps to accomplish your goals. It considers your set priorities (urgency, importance, start date, and terms of completion) to identify your first task automatically.

Conclusion

You can become a master time manager when you practice the techniques and use the tools recommended in this book. Reclaim your time from busywork, have more hours to spend with your loved ones and improve your personal life. The main reason for having improved time management skills is to increase our experience of pleasure, happiness, and the overall quality of our lives. Three things largely determine the quality of your life:

- Inner life
- Health
- Relationships

- **Inner life** involves feeling good about your personality and character, liking yourself and getting along with yourself. It takes time and reflection to improve your inner life.
- **Health.** No level of success is worth having poor health. Most times, the best use of your time involves going to bed early and having a good night's sleep. Also, take time out to get proper rest, exercise regularly, and eat the right foods.
- **Relationships.** Make out time for your loved ones. The most influential people in your life are those you care about and those who care about you. So, don't get caught up in so much at the expense of vital relationships with your loved ones. A balanced life is a great life. You will find greater fulfillment, satisfaction, and joy by enhancing the quality of your life. Let me leave you with the words of a wise old doctor. "Having spoken to lots of people when

they are about to die, no businesses man on his deathbed ever wished to spend more time in his office."

You just learned proven steps and strategies for managing your time efficiently and effectively. That means you can now improve your productivity and achieve your goals. Still, packing away all this information in your head won't do you any good if you don't put it to use. Hence, I encourage you to return to chapter 1 and identify the reasons why you're failing at time management. Then, review the steps in subsequent chapters and start implementing them right away.

When you implement the steps and strategies in this book, you will see a marked improvement in your life. You feel more in control and have more time for yourself. Start every day with an accomplishment that gives you energy. This can be a physical workout or meditation.

At first, implementing these techniques can make you feel uncomfortable. But the rewards can make your day highly productive. You will experience greater confidence because you are more energetic. Once your weekly plans and activities become a habit, challenge yourself to create a monthly plan.

Over time, you should develop a 3-month, 6-month, and an annual plan. Take a weekend off at the end of the year to reflect on the previous year and plan for the new one. Ensure you schedule your events, vacations, and projects into your yearly plan. Planning your future with a well-designed plan can calm your nerves in this world of uncertainty.

When you are in charge of your time, you have improved confidence that's noticeable to others. Saving time involves investing some time to plan, make changes, and improve your life. The most significant single piece of advice I can give you at this point is: do not get lost in the weeds! By this, I mean, do not get lost in every tiny detail.

Getting good at managing your time requires you to take action rather than trying to get every last detail in order. Even if you are feeling unsure about whether or not you're doing things correctly, it is far more important to get started. I can't stress this enough. I promise that results will come with just some practice and some experience. That is the only thing separating you from achieving the goals you desire. Don't worry about whether or not everything is 100% perfect or feeling skeptical whether or not this will work for you. Just do it. All of these excuses will only stunt your growth. Take action now — not tomorrow. Your success depends on the action you take today.

I'm going to challenge you to be accountable. Call a trusted friend and share your goal of better time management. That's right; you're going to be held accountable. Because this time you won't fail. This time you're going to get better at managing your time finally. No matter who you are, you can manage your time with greater efficiency. You deserve this. So, go ahead and get started now, because higher productivity and a better life is waiting for you!

www.ingramcontent.com/pod-product-compliance
Lightning Source LLC
Chambersburg PA
CBHW031126080526
44587CB00011B/1126